Microwave Cooking with Style

Microwave Cooking with Style

Barb Holland and Roxanne McQuilkin

McGraw-Hill Ryerson Limited
Toronto   Montreal

Microwave Cooking with Style

© 1988 Barb Holland Home Economist Inc. and Roxanne McQuilkin

All rights reserved. No part of this publication may be reproduced, stored in a retrieval system, or transmitted, in any form or by any means, electronic, mechanical, photocopying, recording, or otherwise, without prior written permission of McGraw-Hill Ryerson Limited.

ISBN 0-07-549658-5

1 2 3 4 5 6 7 8 9 0   M   7 6 5 4 3 2 1 0 9 8

Care has been taken to trace the ownership of any copyright material contained in this text. The publishers will gladly take any information that will enable them to rectify any reference or credit in subsequent editions.

Printed and bound in Canada

Canadian Cataloguing in Publication Data
Holland, Barb.
  Microwave cooking with style

Includes index.
ISBN 0-07-549658-5

1. Microwave cookery.   I. McQuilkin, Roxanne.
II. Title.

TX832.H64 1988   641.5'882   C88-094260-6

Library of Congress Cataloging-in-Publication Data
Holland, Barb.
    Microwave cooking with style / by Barb Holland and Roxanne
    McQuilkin.
    p. cm.
    Includes index.
    ISBN 0-07-549658-5 : $16.95
    1. Microwave cookery. I. McQuilkin, Roxanne.   II. Title.
TX832.H64 1989
641.5'882—dc19   88-9210

Editorial and design by Abraham Tanaka Associates Limited
Illustrations by Bo-Kim Louie
Cover photograph by G. Biss Photography
Food styling by Barb Holland

To Mike, who introduced me to the computer about the same time I introduced him to the microwave. He is not only my best critic and computer consultant, but has managed, despite it all, to maintain his cool and his slim figure.

Thanks to Iris Raven and Shelley Tanaka for their good measures of common sense which they dispensed so readily. Thanks to the many friends and students who tested and tasted so willingly. Finally, thank you to Denise Schon who made it possible.

Barb Holland

For Mother and Dad, Alan, and friends who supported the cause by tasting and commenting, and Barb for her encouragement.

Roxanne McQuilkin

Contents

Introduction

Like all busy working people, we understand the difficulty of getting meals on the dinner table. Most days this requires the coordination of a juggler, the stamina and perseverance of an Olympic athlete, and some creativity thrown in for good measure. With hectic schedules, the task of producing well-balanced, delicious meals day after day is unnerving for most of us.

Today well over fifty percent of all North American households own microwave ovens, and the numbers are increasing all the time. We know very well why they are purchased—to save time. We also know that they are primarily used for reheating and defrosting.

Certainly the microwave oven is a great timesaver. But many people are surprised to discover that it is also a practical appliance for primary cooking. And that is what this book is all about.

We have developed recipes that we would want to serve to family and friends (and we did many times!), and that are quick and easy to make, look good, but above all are delicious. We have also tried to include many dishes—such as Scallops in Pernod Cream Sauce, Smoked Salmon and Cream Cheese Quiche and Apple Custard Flan—that are special and a little bit different. These are recipes suitable for entertaining your most elegant dinner guests, or your fussiest family!

But we have not included recipes that are inferior microwave-based adaptations of conventional recipes. Our philosophy is to use each kitchen appliance to its maximum. Some of the recipes are quicker-cooking adaptations of popular dishes, but many more have been developed especially for the microwave; they are actually better cooked in the microwave than cooked conventionally.

Unlike many microwave cookbooks, we encourage you to combine appliances. Use the broiler after microwaving for a crisp topping. One of our favorite combinations is the microwave and the barbecue—moist, delicious and faster-cooking in the microwave, plus the flavor and crispness of the barbecue.

Remember, the microwave oven is just one appliance, and while it will do quite a few things, if you expect it to do everything, you will probably be disappointed. And even if you don't understand the chemistry or technology behind cooking, you should easily be able to handle every recipe in this book.

We hope you'll use this cookbook often—that you'll try the recipes and read the microwave tips. Use your microwave oven every day, and soon you'll wonder what you ever did before it came into your kitchen.

Barb Holland and Roxanne McQuilkin

1
Microwave Cooking Basics

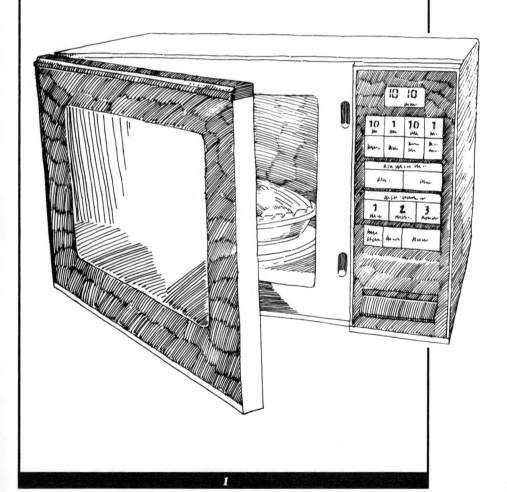

The first step in mastering microwave cooking is to appreciate how it differs from conventional cooking.

Microwaves are a form of electro-magnetic energy that are absorbed by water, fat and sugar molecules. The absorbed micro-wave energy causes the molecules to vibrate very rapidly (2½ billion times per second). When this happens, the friction produces heat, which cooks the food.

This molecular action continues even when there is no longer microwave energy. This is known as "standing time" or "carry-over cooking," which allows the carry-over heat to continue cooking through to the center of the food by conduction.

Conventional cooking works by a similar molecular action. However, heat is first initiated from the element or flame, then transferred to the cooking container and finally to the food. Microwaves immediately penetrate the outer edges of food ½ to 1½ inches (1 to 4 cm), depending on the density of the food. The food is then cooked from these outer edges through to the center by conduction. Only then does the heated food heat up the dish and oven cavity—the reverse of conventional cooking.

Moving in straight lines, microwaves form a pattern as they bounce off the metal walls. Various forms of stirrer blades and turn-tables are used to even out this cooking pattern. Turning, rotating, stirring and shielding are additional techniques to help produce even cooking results.

Microwave energy will vary from oven to oven. The recipes in this book were developed and tested for 600 to 700 watt microwave ovens. A lower wattage oven may require additional cooking time, while a higher wattage oven may need less cooking time. The recipes use the following standard terms for power levels as established by the International Microwave Power Institute:

High	(100%)
Medium-High	(70%)
Medium	(50%)
Medium-Low	(30%)
Low	(10%)

Some microwave manufacturers use different names for different power levels. If you are unsure about the cooking wattage or power levels of your microwave oven, consult the instruction manual provided with the oven.

Just as all foods are not cooked at maximum heat in conventional cooking, the different power levels in a microwave provide the flexibility to cook a wide range of foods. For example, vegetables and chicken are usually microwaved at High (100%); cheesecakes and quiches at Medium (50%); and custards and other egg dishes at Medium-Low (30%).

Read the introductory section of your oven's instruction manual or cookbook to become familiar with the functions, features and safety procedures of your oven. Only by *using* your microwave oven will you really understand how often to turn, rotate and rearrange food. Your microwave oven is as individual as you are. Knowing more about your oven's finer points will help you get the most from this amazing appliance.

As in conventional cooking, the starting temperature affects the total cooking time—frozen and refrigerated foods will take longer to cook than food at room temperature. But unlike conventional cooking, microwave cooking has a number of other variables that influence the cooking time and results.

Quantity of Food

More food means more cooking time. The more food you put in the microwave oven, the more microwave energy is needed to work on the additional moisture, fat and sugar molecules; therefore, a longer cooking time is required.

Size and Shape

For even cooking, cut meat and vegetables into pieces of uniform size and shape, whenever possible—1 inch (2.5 cm) cubes are ideal. Because microwaves penetrate from every angle, round or ring shapes produce more evenly cooked food than square and rectangular shapes.

Composition of Food

Dense food such as meat will take longer to cook than less dense foods of equal size. Microwaves are attracted to sugar and fat, so these foods get hot much more quickly than those high in water, and they tend to reach the boiling point more quickly.

Cooking Techniques

Stirring and Turning

Foods are stirred for the same reasons in microwave cooking as in conventional cooking—to distribute the heated parts. But turning food over partway through cooking is also necessary for large, dense items like a whole chicken or roast. As a general rule, foods that are over 2 inches (5 cm) thick (whole squash, roasts, etc.) should be turned over partway through cooking.

Arrangement

Positioning food in a spoke fashion, with thick parts at the outer edges of the dish, takes advantage of the nature of microwave cooking. (Most ovens cook from the outer edges to the center. However, cooking patterns can vary from oven to oven—note the pattern of your oven to determine whether cooking is faster on the outside or in the center.) Arrange pieces of food in the cooking dish in a circle. For example, arrange whole potatoes in a circle, leaving a few inches in between each potato, and the center of the circle empty. Arrange drumsticks or chops with the meatier portions to the outer edges of the dish. Spreading food out in a single layer rather than piling it up allows the microwaves to affect a larger surface area, so the cooking will be more efficient and even.

Covering

As a general rule, the foods you would cover when cooking conventionally should also be covered in a microwave. Covering helps food cook more quickly and evenly and prevents splattering.

Covers or lids that match the dish are ideal, particularly when you want to retain as much moisture as possible when steaming or poaching. Microwavable plastic wrap is another alternative—turn back a small edge of the wrap to allow excess steam to escape, and to prevent boilovers and splitting.

Waxed or parchment paper can also be used to hold in heat and prevent splattering. Tuck it around the food to keep it in place. Plain white, pure (not recycled) paper towels absorb moisture and help to prevent sogginess when cooking bacon or heating sandwiches.

Piercing

When cooking foods with a skin or membrane, such as whole potatoes, squash, chicken and whole fish, pierce the skin to allow steam to escape. Otherwise, messy ruptures can occur.

Salting

Salt attracts microwaves, so food will overcook in areas where salt lies on the surface. Microwave cooking also tends to intensify flavors, so be subtle with seasonings.

Shielding

Microwaves reflect off metal. Small pieces of aluminum foil can be used for shielding to prevent overcooking, particularly when cooking uneven or square shapes. Avoid placing foil or metal within 1 inch (2.5 cm) of the oven walls or another piece of foil. Otherwise, arcing may occur. Arcing is a spark or discharge of electricity between two metal points. It looks like lightning or a blue spark in your microwave. If it occurs, quickly turn off the microwave and remove the offending piece of foil, metal-rimmed dish or other object. Check your oven manual and follow its recommendation regarding the use of foil.

Standing Time

Probably the most important microwave technique and the least understood is standing time or carry-over cooking. Foods continue to cook, even after the microwave has been turned off—from a few minutes to as long as 20 minutes. Standing time depends on the cooking time, power level used, density and type of food cooked. The standing time allows the food to continue cooking through by conduction. Large dense items like roast chicken or whole rutabaga should be wrapped or covered with foil during standing time. This actually helps to increase the internal temperature. Shorter-cooking or less dense items usually require a shorter standing time, and are just covered to finish the cooking.

During standing time, dishes should be placed on the counter and kept warm with a lid or folded terry towel. Do not cover foods that are cooked uncovered, such as cakes. Cakes should, however, stand on the counter or a flat surface rather than a rack to complete the cooking.

Microwave Cookware

There are many types of cookware that can be used for microwave cooking; only a few cannot. Suitable microwave cookware allows the microwave energy to pass through the cookware material with minimal absorption, tolerates temperatures reached in microwave cooking, especially those of fats and sugars, and is made of material approved for contact with food.

Approved materials include glass, glass-ceramic, pottery, ceramics (earthenware, stoneware, fine china), microwavable plastic and paper. However, some pottery and china may include a type of clay or glaze that absorbs microwave energy, causing the dish to become hot. Metal pans, or plates and dishes with metallic trim or decoration, should not be used in the microwave.

To determine if what you have in your kitchen cupboard is suitable for use in the microwave, place a glass measure filled with 1 cup (250 mL) water in the microwave oven. Place the dish to be tested near but not touching the measure. Microwave at High (100%) for 1 minute. If the dish is cool, it is safe for microwaving; if it is warm, it may be used for reheating foods. But if it is hot, it is absorbing too much microwave energy for efficient cooking and should not be used.

Not all plastic is acceptable for microwave use. Be sure to use plastic cookware that has been specified by the manufacturer as being microwavable. There are many types now available in a large range of shapes and sizes. Some can go from freezer to microwave (or conventional oven) to dishwasher.

Plastic storage containers such as those used for margarine or yogurt are not intended to tolerate cooking temperatures, and are not suitable for use in the microwave.

Paper plates and towels can be used for simple cooking or reheating, but avoid recycled paper products, as they may contain small amounts of metal. Colored paper towels or napkins are not recommended, as the dye could run.

Wicker and straw baskets (without metal parts) can be used to heat breads and rolls. Wooden utensils such as wooden spoons can be left in foods for short cooking times, as when stirring a sauce.

A Word About Common Sense

Despite the fact that you are working with an electronically operated appliance that is often accurate to the second, when a dish looks like it's boiling over or drying out, stop cooking it. Consider other clues that you have been using when cooking conventionally. Aroma will change as food cooks; color also changes in some foods. And sometimes you can even hear changes—the sound of something exploding is an excellent indication that cooking should be stopped!

In general, be aware of the variables, use common sense and check the food regularly as it is cooking, particularly if you are new to microwave cooking. Your confidence will grow the more you use your microwave; eventually you will learn how your particular oven works, and constant attention will not be necessary.

2
Appetizers

Whether you are serving finger food with drinks, or a starter to an elegant meal, the microwave can cut your work considerably when you are preparing appetizers. Because the microwave heats without drying, it has the advantage of allowing you to prepare many of these dishes ahead of time and then reheating them just before serving. And many appetizers, such as those containing bacon or seafood, are actually better cooked in the microwave, since seafood remains moist and the bacon crisps nicely.

Many attractive serving dishes are microwavable and ideal for reheating and serving appetizers. However, you may want to just reheat on these special platters, as they can become hot and messy if food is actually cooked on them.

Included in this chapter are finger foods, nibblers and dips ideal for a cocktail party, as well as appetizers suitable for serving at the table to precede the main course. Other appetizer suggestions can be found in Soups, The Lighter Side and Gifts from the Kitchen.

Country Terrine with Fresh Tomato Salsa

This country-style pâté is ideal for picnics, sandwiches or buffets. Make it a few days ahead so the flavors will blend. Slice thinly and serve with French bread, gherkins, and either a crock of Dijon mustard or Fresh Tomato Salsa. The exact proportions are not important, but the total weight of the meat should be about 2 lb (1 kg).

8 oz	uncooked turkey	250 g
6 oz	cooked ham	180 g
10 oz	ground pork	300 g
10 oz	ground veal	300 g
1	clove garlic, minced	1
1	onion, finely chopped	1
¼ cup	pine nuts	50 mL
1 tsp	salt	5 mL
1 tsp	freshly ground black pepper	5 mL
1 tsp	dried rosemary	5 mL
½ cup	beef stock	125 mL
2 tbsp	finely chopped parsley	25 mL

▶ Coarsely grind or chop turkey and ham in food processor or with a sharp knife.

▶ In large bowl, combine all ingredients well. Pack into a micro-wavable 9 × 5 inch (2 L) loaf pan. Cover with waxed paper. Micro-wave at Medium-High (70%) for 25 to 30 minutes, or until internal temperature reaches 160 F (70 C). Do not drain.

▶ Cover terrine with plastic wrap and weight the top with a small board or box and moderately heavy cans or other weights. Allow to cool.

▶ Refrigerate for 2 to 3 days, but remove the weight after 24 hours. Unmold, scrape off congealed fat and let stand for 30 minutes at room temperature before slicing.

Makes 10 to 16 servings

Fresh Tomato Salsa

This uncooked sauce has a cool, fresh flavor.
Use very ripe tomatoes for maximum flavor.

4	ripe tomatoes, peeled, seeded and chopped	4
1	onion, chopped	1
2 tbsp	finely chopped parsley	25 mL
2 tbsp	red wine vinegar	25 mL
1 tsp	granulated sugar	5 mL
¼ cup	vegetable or olive oil	50 mL
	Salt and freshly ground black pepper to taste	

▶ Combine all ingredients.

Makes about 2 cups (500 mL)

Dilled Ricotta Torte

A nicely textured cheese dish with a hint of lemon and pepper. It can be made up to two days ahead and served warm, at room temperature or chilled. Cut in wedges and garnish with fresh dill or lemon slices.

CRUST

¼ cup	butter	50 mL
1 cup	dry dark rye breadcrumbs	250 mL
1 cup	sliced almonds	250 mL

FILLING

3	eggs	3
3 cups	ricotta cheese	750 mL
2 tbsp	chopped fresh dill, or 1 tsp (5 mL) dried dill weed	25 mL
½ tsp	salt	2 mL
½ tsp	freshly ground black pepper	2 mL
	Grated rind of ½ lemon	

▶ To make crust, in a round 9 inch (23 cm) glass cake dish, melt butter at High (100%) for 40 to 60 seconds. Stir in crumbs and almonds and coat evenly with butter. Pat along sides and bottom of dish. Microwave at High (100%) for 2 to 3 minutes, or until firm to the touch. Set aside.

▶ To make filling, in large bowl, beat eggs. Add remaining filling ingredients, stirring until smooth. Pour into prepared crust.

▶ Microwave, uncovered, at Medium-High (70%) for 12 to 15 minutes, or until just set in the center. Let stand directly on counter for 10 minutes before serving, or cool to room temperature.

Makes 12 to 16 appetizer servings

TIP To dry lemon or orange rind, place the grated rind of one orange or lemon on flat microwavable plate. Cover with a paper towel and microwave at High (100%) for 30 to 60 seconds, or until dry. Stir once during cooking.

Breaded Chicken Fingers with Three Dipping Sauces

The light coating of flour, egg and seasoned breadcrumbs keeps the chicken moist and crisp. These are lighter and juicier than commercial nuggets. Children love them, and you avoid the calories and trouble of deep-frying. Serve with one, two or all three of the sauces. Make them ahead and serve warm or at room temperature.

1 lb	boned and skinned chicken breasts	500 g
1	egg	1
1 tbsp	water	15 mL
½ cup	dry breadcrumbs	125 mL
¼ cup	cornmeal	50 mL
2 tbsp	grated Parmesan cheese	25 mL
1 tsp	paprika	5 mL
½ tsp	salt	2 mL
1½ tsp	garlic powder	2 mL
½ tsp	freshly ground black pepper	2 mL
½ tsp	dried thyme or basil	2 mL
¼ tsp	dried oregano	1 mL
¼ cup	all-purpose flour	50 mL

▶ Slice the chicken into ½ inch (1 cm) strips. Set aside.
▶ Combine egg and water in a shallow dish or pie plate.
▶ Make coating mixture by combining breadcrumbs, cornmeal, Parmesan and seasonings in another shallow dish.
▶ Coat the chicken fingers with flour a few pieces at a time and shake off excess.
▶ Dip chicken in the egg mixture, then in breadcrumb mixture.
▶ Arrange the chicken evenly on a microwave roasting rack. You may have to do this in two batches to avoid crowding the chicken fingers.
▶ Microwave, uncovered, at High (100%) for 4 to 6 minutes, or until the juices run clear, with no trace of pink, when the chicken is pierced. Let stand for a few minutes before serving. If you cook the chicken in two batches, divide the cooking time accordingly. Do not overcook.

Makes 8 to 10 appetizer servings

Plum Dipping Sauce

½ cup	plum jam or jelly	125 mL
1	clove garlic, minced	1
1 tsp	grated fresh ginger	5 mL
¼ cup	white vinegar	50 mL
1 tbsp	soy sauce	15 mL
1 tsp	cornstarch	5 mL

▶ Combine all ingredients in a 2 cup (500 mL) glass measure. Microwave, uncovered, at High (100%), or for 2 to 3 minutes until sauce comes to a boil and thickens. Stir partway through cooking.

Makes ¾ cup (175 mL)

Honey Mustard Sauce

2 tbsp	dry mustard	25 mL
¼ cup	granulated sugar	50 mL
¼ cup	white vinegar	50 mL
2 tbsp	honey	25 mL
pinch	salt	pinch

▶ In a 2 cup (500 mL) glass measure, combine the mustard and sugar until smooth. Stir in remaining ingredients.
▶ Microwave, uncovered, at High (100%) for 1 to 2 minutes, or until sauce boils and thickens. Stir well.

Makes ½ cup (125 mL)

Hot Sauce

2 tbsp	butter	25 mL
1	small onion, finely chopped	1
1	clove garlic, minced	1
½ cup	ketchup	125 mL
2 tbsp	lemon juice	25 mL
½ tsp	Tabasco	2 mL

▶ Combine the butter, onion and garlic in a 2 cup (500 mL) glass measure. Microwave, uncovered, at High (100%) for 1 to 2 minutes, or until soft.

▶ Add ketchup, lemon juice and Tabasco. Stir well. Taste and add more Tabasco if you wish.

Makes ¾ cup (175 mL)

Jalapeño Cheese Dip

A cheese dip with lots of kick. Use four jalapeño peppers if you like it hot, two or three if you prefer it milder. If you are using canned jalapeño peppers, drain and rinse them before chopping. This dip is best served warm. Use tortilla chips or raw vegetables as dippers. If you are pressed for time, make ahead, cover and refrigerate. Reheat, covered, at Medium (50%) until warm and stir until smooth.

1	onion, chopped	1
1	clove garlic, minced	1
2 to 4	jalapeño peppers, seeded and diced	2 to 4
1 tbsp	vegetable oil	15 mL
1½ cups	grated old Cheddar cheese	375 mL
1½ cups	grated brick cheese	375 mL
¼ cup	milk	50 mL

▶ Combine onion, garlic, jalapeño peppers and oil in a 4 cup (1 L) microwavable casserole. Microwave, uncovered, at High (100%) for 2 to 3 minutes, or until onion and peppers are softened.

▶ Stir in cheeses and milk. Cover and microwave at Medium (50%) for 2 to 3 minutes, or until cheese has melted. Stir at least once partway through cooking to help melt cheese. Stir until smooth. If dip is thicker than you would like, stir in more milk.

▶ Serve with tortilla chips or raw vegetables.

Makes 4 to 6 servings

Chicken Satays
with Peanut Sauce

This popular appetizer from southeast Asia can also be made with pork or shrimp.

6	chicken breasts, skinned and boned	6
¼ cup	soy sauce	50 mL
2 tbsp	lime juice	25 mL
1 tbsp	vegetable oil	15 mL
1 tbsp	brown sugar	15 mL
1	small onion, chopped	1
2	cloves garlic, minced	2
½ tsp	hot red pepper flakes	2 mL

▶ Cut chicken into 1 inch (2.5 cm) pieces. In a bowl just large enough to hold chicken pieces, combine soy sauce, lime juice, oil, brown sugar, onion, garlic and hot pepper flakes. Toss chicken in mixture to coat. Cover and marinate in the refrigerator for 2 to 4 hours. Meanwhile, make Peanut Sauce, cover and set aside.

▶ Thread chicken pieces on 12 bamboo skewers, leaving a small space between each piece for even cooking. Arrange 6 skewers on a microwave roasting rack, spacing out evenly. Cover with waxed paper and microwave at Medium-High (70%) for 6 to 8 minutes, or until tender and no longer pink. Repeat with remaining 6 skewers. Serve with Peanut Sauce.

Serves 6

Peanut Sauce

½ cup	smooth peanut butter	125 mL
½ cup	water	125 mL
2 tbsp	soy sauce	25 mL
¼ cup	lime juice	50 mL
3	green onions, finely chopped	3
½ tsp	hot red pepper flakes	2 mL

▶ In a 2 cup (500 mL) glass measure, combine all sauce ingredients. Microwave, uncovered, at High (100%) for 1½ to 2 minutes, or until sauce is smooth. Stir partway through cooking. Stir again until smooth and cool to room temperature. Sauce will thicken slightly as it cools. Serve at room temperature. If sauce is too thick, thin with water, blending well.

Makes about 1 cup (250 mL)

Rumaki

Like most bacon-wrapped dishes, this traditional appetizer does well in the microwave, as the bacon crisps up evenly, without burning.

8 oz	chicken livers	250 g
1	10 oz (284 mL) can water chestnuts	1
12	slices bacon, cut in half	12
¼ cup	soy sauce	50 mL
2 tbsp	dry sherry	25 mL
1 tbsp	brown sugar	15 mL
2	cloves garlic, minced	2
½ tsp	grated fresh ginger	2 mL

▶ Trim chicken livers of excess fat and membranes, and cut into 24 pieces. Drain water chestnuts, rinse and cut into 24 pieces.
▶ Wrap a piece of bacon around a piece of chicken liver and water chestnut. Secure with a toothpick. Repeat with the remaining. Arrange in one layer in a shallow dish.
▶ Combine remaining ingredients in cup and spoon evenly over rumaki. Cover and refrigerate for at least 1 hour.
▶ Arrange half the rumaki on a microwave roasting rack, about 1 inch (2.5 cm) apart. Microwave, uncovered, at High (100%) for 6 to 8 minutes, or until liver is cooked and bacon is crisp. Repeat with remaining rumaki. Serve warm.

Makes 24 appetizers

Salmon Balls
with Horseradish Sauce

A quick appetizer for a cocktail party. Use red salmon for the best color. This dish is best served warm or at room temperature. Provide cocktail forks and pass with the sauce.
If you are making the salmon balls ahead of time, cover and refrigerate. Before serving, reheat, uncovered, at Medium-High (70%) for 2 to 3 minutes, or until warm. If you don't have leftover mashed potatoes, pierce a medium potato and microwave, uncovered, at High (100%) for 3 to 5 minutes, or until tender. Let stand for a few minutes before peeling and mashing with a fork.

1	7½ oz (213 g) can red salmon	1
1	small onion, finely chopped	1
1	egg, lightly beaten	1
½ cup	mashed potatoes	125 mL
1 tbsp	grated Parmesan cheese	15 mL
½ tsp	dried dill weed	2 mL
	Freshly ground black pepper to taste	

▶ Drain salmon and break up in medium bowl. Stir in remaining ingredients until evenly blended.
▶ Form mixture into 1 inch (2.5 cm) balls. The mixture will be soft, but will firm up during cooking. Place in circular pattern in a shallow dish or plate. Leave center of plate empty. Microwave, uncovered, at High (100%) for 3 to 4 minutes, or until firm. Let stand for 5 minutes before serving.

Makes 20 to 25 balls

Horseradish Sauce

2 tbsp	butter	25 mL
2 tbsp	all-purpose flour	25 mL
⅔ cup	chicken stock	150 mL
¼ cup	horseradish	50 mL

1 tsp	granulated sugar	5 mL
½ cup	sour cream	125 mL
	Salt and freshly ground black pepper to taste	

▶ In a 2 cup (500 mL) glass measure, combine butter and flour. Microwave at High (100%) for 30 to 60 seconds, or until butter has melted. Stir with a fork to combine well.

▶ Whisk in stock and microwave, uncovered, at High (100%) for 2 to 3 minutes, or until mixture comes to a boil and thickens. Stir twice during cooking.

▶ Stir in horseradish, sugar and sour cream. Season to taste with salt and pepper. Serve warm with Salmon Balls.

Makes 1¼ cups (300 mL)

Brie Melt

An easy appetizer to put together at the last minute. Buy the Brie at a store you know has a high turnover. Old Brie has a strong, astringent taste. If you prefer a milder taste, buy Canadian Brie. Use slices of tart green apple, pears or whole strawberries as dippers. If the dip cools and solidifies before all is eaten, just reheat it at Medium (50%) until runny again.

8 oz	Brie cheese	250 g
1 tbsp	brown sugar	15 mL
1 tbsp	sliced almonds	15 mL
	Fresh apple or pear slices, whole strawberries, crackers or bread sticks	

▶ Remove rind from Brie and cut cheese into cubes. Place in a small microwavable dish or bowl just slightly larger than the Brie (the cheese will melt down when cooked). Sprinkle with brown sugar and almonds.

▶ Microwave, uncovered, at Medium (50%) for 2 to 3 minutes, stirring twice during cooking, until cheese melts and is runny.

Serves 4 to 6

Curried Crab and Artichoke Canapés

Wonton wrappers make crisp, light cups for this colorful appetizer. The wrappers can be found in the produce department of many supermarkets, and the cups are very easy to make. Both the cups and the filling can be made ahead, then assembled before serving.

18	wonton wrappers	18
1 tbsp	butter	15 mL
1	small stalk celery, chopped	1
3	green onions, chopped	3
1 tsp	curry powder	5 mL
½ tsp	ground cumin	2 mL
pinch	cayenne	pinch
1 tsp	lemon juice	5 mL
1	4¼ oz (120 g) can crab meat, drained and shredded	1
1	6 oz (170 mL) jar marinated artichoke hearts, well drained and chopped	1
1 to 2 tbsp	mayonnaise or Creamy Salad Dressing (page 136)	15 to 25 mL
2 tbsp	finely chopped parsley	25 mL

▶ Separate wonton wrappers and place individually in microwavable muffin pan or custard cups to form cups. Microwave, uncovered, 6 cups at a time at High (100%) for 1 to 1½ minutes, or until wrappers are opaque and light-brown in color (check underside). Rotate pan, if necessary, during cooking. Remove cups immediately to a wire rack to cool and crisp. Dry moisture from muffin pan and continue with remaining wrappers.

▶ In a 4 cup (1 L) microwavable casserole or bowl, combine butter, celery and green onions. Microwave, uncovered, at High (100%) for 1 to 2 minutes, to partially soften celery.

▶ Stir in curry powder, cumin and cayenne. Microwave, uncovered, at High (100%) for 1 minute. Stir in lemon juice, crab meat and artichoke hearts. Cover and microwave at High (100%) for 2 to 3 minutes, or until warm.

▶ Stir in just enough mayonnaise to hold mixture together. Spoon filling into wonton cups. Sprinkle with chopped parsley and serve immediately.

Makes 18 appetizers

Cajun Shrimp

This spicy dish is best served warm and with plenty of cold beer. It can also be served as a meal over cooked rice and with a green vegetable or salad.

¼ cup	butter	50 mL
4	green onions, sliced	4
2	cloves garlic, minced	2
1 lb	raw shrimp, peeled and deveined	500 g
½ 1 tsp	cayenne	5 mL
½ tsp	paprika	2 mL
½ tsp	dried thyme	2 mL
½ tsp	dried oregano	2 mL
¼ tsp	salt	1 mL
¼ tsp	freshly ground black pepper	1 mL

Prepare ahead

▶ Combine butter, green onions and garlic in an 8 cup (2 L) microwavable casserole. Microwave, uncovered, at High (100%) for 2 minutes. Stir in shrimp, coating well with butter mixture.

▶ In small bowl or cup, combine seasonings. Sprinkle evenly over shrimp and toss well again. Cover and microwave at Medium-High (70%) for 5 to 7 minutes, stirring gently at least once during cooking, until shrimp are opaque. Do not overcook. Let stand for 5 minutes before serving.

Makes 8 to 10 appetizer servings, or 4 main-course servings

Shrimp in Ginger Sauce

The preserved ginger gives the shrimp zip and some sweetness. Use medium-sized shrimp—the large ones are too big for appetizers.

⅓ cup	dry white wine	75 mL
2 tbsp	lemon juice	25 mL
1 tbsp	soy sauce	15 mL
1 tbsp	syrup from preserved ginger	15 mL
2	pieces preserved or stem ginger, slivered	2
3	green onions, chopped	3
1 lb	raw shrimp, unpeeled	500 g
1 tbsp	brown sugar	15 mL
1 tsp	cornstarch	5 mL

▶ In an 8 cup (2 L) microwavable casserole, combine wine, lemon juice, soy sauce, ginger syrup, ginger and green onions. Cover with lid or vented plastic wrap and microwave at High (100%) for 2 to 3 minutes, or until mixture boils.

▶ Add shrimp, cover and microwave at High (100%) for 4 to 6 minutes, stirring at least once partway through cooking. Cook just until shrimp are pink and opaque. Let stand for a few minutes.

▶ Remove shrimp with a slotted spoon. When cool enough to handle, remove shells and devein. Set aside.

▶ Stir brown sugar into liquid in casserole. Mix a small amount of the liquid with cornstarch in a cup. Stir until smooth, then pour back into sauce mixture. Cover and microwave at High (100%) for 1 to 2 minutes, stirring partway through, until mixture comes to a boil and thickens.

▶ Add shrimp to sauce, mixing gently to coat shrimp. Serve warm with cocktail picks.

Makes 8 to 10 appetizer servings

TIP To soften a chip or vegetable dip that has become firm in the refrigerator, transfer 1 cup (250 mL) dip to a microwavable cup or bowl. Stir a spoonful or two of liquid (milk or other main ingredient) into the dip and microwave, uncovered, at Medium-High (70%) for 1 to 1½ minutes, or until softened. Stir often.

Mussels in Curry Cream Broth

These mussels are so good, you'll want to make an entire meal of them. Serve with crusty Italian bread for dipping into the broth, and have empty bowls on the table for the shells.

2 lb	mussels	1 kg
1 tbsp	butter	15 mL
4	green onions, chopped	4
1	clove garlic, minced	1
2 tsp	curry powder	10 mL
1	tomato, seeded and chopped	1
2 tbsp	finely chopped parsley	25 mL
½ tsp	salt	2 mL
½ tsp	freshly ground black pepper	2 mL
½ tsp	dried oregano	2 mL
1½ cups	dry white wine	375 mL
½ cup	whipping cream	125 mL

▶ Soak mussels in salted water for 1 hour before cleaning and cooking. Scrub the shells with a stiff brush and remove the beards. Discard any mussels that will not close tightly when tapped, or any with cracked or broken shells.

▶ Combine butter, onions, garlic and curry powder in a 16 cup (4 L) microwavable casserole. Microwave, uncovered, at High (100%) for 2 minutes, stirring once.

▶ Add tomato and microwave, uncovered, at High (100%) for 1 to 2 minutes, or until vegetables are tender. Add parsley, salt, pepper, oregano and wine. Cover and microwave at High (100%) for 2 to 3 minutes, or until hot.

▶ Add mussels, cover and microwave at High (100%) for 10 to 15 minutes, or until the shells have opened. Stir two or three times during cooking. Discard any mussels that have not opened.

▶ Divide mussels between individual serving bowls. Stir cream into broth and pour over each bowl of mussels.

Makes 4 appetizer servings, or 2 main-course servings

Stuffed Mushrooms

*Try a variety of fillings in these stuffed mushrooms. The fillings are
ideal for using up small amounts of leftovers.*

12 to 14	large fresh mushrooms	12 to 14
1 tbsp	butter	15 mL

Mexican Filling

⅓ cup	grated farmer's or brick cheese	75 mL
¼ cup	crushed corn chips	50 mL
¼ cup	finely chopped cooked chicken or turkey	50 mL
2 tbsp	chopped jalapeño peppers	25 mL

Blue Cheese and Pecan Filling

4 oz	cream cheese, softened	125 g
2 tbsp	crumbled blue cheese	25 mL
2 tbsp	chopped pecans	25 mL

Ricotta and Prosciutto Filling

½ cup	ricotta cheese	125 mL
¼ cup	grated Parmesan cheese	50 mL
2	thin slices prosciutto, chopped	2

Smoked Salmon Filling

4 oz	cream cheese, softened	125 g
¼ cup	chopped smoked salmon	50 mL
1 tsp	lemon juice	5 mL
1 tsp	chopped fresh dill, or ½ tsp (2 mL) dried dill weed	5 mL
	Freshly ground black pepper to taste	

Smoked Oyster Filling

4 oz	cream cheese, softened	125 g
4	smoked oysters, drained and chopped	4
2	green onions, chopped	2
1 tsp	lemon juice	5 mL
dash	Tabasco	dash

▶ Clean mushrooms completely. Remove stems right at the base. If cap is not deep enough, scoop out with the tip of a small spoon.
▶ In a small microwavable bowl, melt butter at High (100%) for 30 seconds. Brush tops of caps with butter.
▶ In small bowl, combine desired filling ingredients until smooth. Divide mixture between mushroom caps, about 1 tbsp (15 mL) per cap. Place mushrooms stem side up in a circle on a microwave roasting rack.
▶ Microwave, uncovered, at Medium (50%) for 4 to 7 minutes, or until heated through. Let stand for 3 minutes before serving.

Each recipe makes 12 to 14 appetizers

TIP To open fresh oysters more easily, arrange six in a circle in a glass pie plate. Cover with vented plastic wrap and microwave at High (100%) for about 45 seconds, or just until shells begin to open.

Sticky Chicken Wings

Microwaved chicken wings are moist and tender—perfect finger food. Provide finger bowls with a slice of lemon (heated in the microwave, of course!) or hot damp towels for your guests.

12	chicken wings, about 2 lb (1 kg)	12
¼ cup	hoisin sauce	50 mL
2 tbsp	rice wine or sherry	25 mL
1 tbsp	lemon juice	15 mL
3	cloves garlic, minced	3
1 tbsp	ground cumin	15 mL
1 tsp	granulated sugar	5 mL
½ tsp	cayenne	2 mL

▶ Trim off wing tips and reserve for making stock. Cut between wing joint with a heavy knife or cleaver. You should have 24 pieces in all.

▶ Combine remaining ingredients in a bowl large enough to hold the wings, or in a leak-proof plastic bag. Toss in wings to coat evenly. Cover and refrigerate overnight, stirring occasionally.
▶ Drain wings from marinade and arrange 12 pieces evenly on a microwave roasting rack. Cover with waxed paper and microwave at High (100%) for 4 to 6 minutes, or until juices run clear when pierced. Let stand for 5 to 10 minutes.
▶ Repeat with remaining wings. For a crisper skin, preheat broiler or barbecue. After standing time, transfer all wings to a broiler rack or grill and grill for a couple of minutes until crisp.

Makes 24 pieces, or 4 to 6 appetizer servings

Caponata

A thick Mediterranean-inspired mixture, best made ahead to allow the flavors to blend. Serve cold as a spread on chunks of crusty bread.

4 cups	peeled and finely diced eggplant	1 L
1 cup	finely chopped celery	250 mL
¾ cup	finely chopped onion	175 mL
¼ cup	olive oil	50 mL
2 cups	canned plum tomatoes, chopped and drained	500 mL
¼ cup	tomato paste	50 mL
1 tbsp	red wine vinegar	15 mL
2 tbsp	capers	25 mL
6	black olives, chopped	6
1 tsp	granulated sugar	5 mL
	Freshly ground black pepper to taste	
3	anchovy fillets, or 1 tsp (5 mL) anchovy paste	3
¼ cup	finely chopped parsley	50 mL
2 tbsp	pine nuts	25 mL

▶ Combine eggplant, celery, onion and oil in an 8 cup (2 L) microwavable casserole. Cook, uncovered, at High (100%) for 8 to 10 minutes, or until eggplant is soft. Stir once during cooking time.

▶ Add tomatoes, tomato paste, vinegar, capers, olives, sugar and a generous grating of black pepper. Pound anchovy fillets with a mortar and pestle and stir into mixture, or use anchovy paste.

▶ Cook, uncovered, at High (100%) for 10 to 15 minutes, or until mixture is thick. Stir once during cooking. Stir in parsley and pine nuts. Cool. Serve with chunks of crusty bread.

Makes 4 cups (1 L)

TIP After serving chicken wings or ribs, add a slice of lemon to water in microwavable finger bowls. Microwave at High (100%) for 1 minute per ½ cup (125 mL), or until warm. Or steam damp finger towels at High (100%) for 15 seconds each.

Eggplant Spread

Cooking an eggplant whole in the microwave keeps the flesh an amazing green color and prevents the eggplant from tasting bitter. (When it is cooked conventionally, eggplant usually requires salting and draining in a colander to remove the bitterness.) Make this spread ahead and chill. Serve with small pita breads or sesame crackers.

1	eggplant, about 1 lb (500 g)	1
1	onion, chopped	1
2	cloves garlic, minced	2
2 to 4 tbsp	olive oil	25 to 50 mL
1	ripe tomato, peeled, seeded and chopped	1
2 tbsp	lemon juice	25 mL
1 tsp	granulated sugar	5 mL
½ tsp	salt	2 mL
¼ tsp	freshly ground black pepper	1 mL

▶ Wash and dry eggplant, keeping stem intact. Pierce in several places with a fork. Place on paper towel or on a microwavable plate. Microwave at High (100%) for 5 to 7 minutes, or until tender when pierced with a fork or knife. Let stand until it softens and partially collapses.

▶ Meanwhile combine onion, garlic and 1 tbsp (15 mL) oil in a small microwavable bowl. Microwave, uncovered, at High (100%) for 2 to 4 minutes, or until onion is soft. Stir once during cooking.

▶ Cut eggplant in half lengthwise. With a spoon, scoop out flesh. Discard skin.

▶ Combine eggplant, onion mixture, 1 tbsp (15 mL) oil, tomato, lemon juice, sugar, salt and pepper in a food processor or blender. Process until smooth. Add more oil only if mixture is too thick to spread. Cover and chill until serving time. Serve with small pita breads or sesame crackers.

Makes 1½ cups (375 mL)

Asparagus Maltaise

This elegant, Italian-inspired appetizer uses egg whites in a simple and practical way to create a colorful garnish. If you use lemon juice instead of the orange juice, this becomes Asparagus Hollandaise.

3	eggs, separated	3
1 lb	fresh asparagus	500 g
¼ cup	water	50 mL
¼ cup	butter	50 mL
¼ cup	fresh orange juice	50 mL
pinch	cayenne	pinch
2 tbsp	diced red pepper, optional	25 mL

▶ Place egg whites in a 2 cup (500 mL) glass measure and gently stir so that they will not erupt while cooking. Cover with vented plastic wrap and microwave at Medium-High (70%) for 1 to 1½ minutes, or just until firm. Gently stir twice during cooking. Set aside to cool, then chop finely.

▶ Snap off tough ends of asparagus. Place in a shallow microwavable dish in a single layer, arranging stalks toward outer edges of dish. Pour water over asparagus and cover with vented plastic wrap.

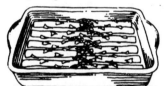

▶ Microwave at High (100%) for 4 to 6 minutes, or until asparagus is bright green. Let stand, covered, while making sauce.

▶ In small bowl or cup, lightly beat egg yolks. Set aside.

▶ In a 2 cup (500 mL) glass measure, melt butter at High (100%) for 40 to 60 seconds. Do not let butter bubble, or it will be too hot to add to the egg yolks. Stir orange juice into butter, then beat egg yolks into butter mixture.

▶ Microwave, uncovered, at Medium-Low (30%) for 1 to 2 minutes, or until sauce thickens. Whisk sauce every 30 seconds during cooking. Do not overcook sauce, or it will curdle. Season with cayenne.

▶ Spoon some sauce on individual warm plates. Arrange a serving of asparagus in a fan design over the sauce. Sprinkle with chopped egg white and red pepper.

Makes 4 servings

Steamed Artichokes with Hollandaise Sauce

Artichokes will steam in the microwave in at least half the time of conventional cooking, while retaining their beautiful color. You can also cook artichokes this way before stuffing them.
To eat, pull each leaf out by the tip and dip the fleshy end into the sauce. Once the leaves are finished, cut the heart into wedges and dip into the sauce.

4	medium artichokes	4
½	lemon	½
¼ cup	water	50 mL
	Hollandaise Sauce (page 134)	

▶ Remove tough outer leaves of artichokes. Cut off the stems to allow artichokes to stand upright. With scissors, cut ½ inch (1 cm) off the tip of each leaf. Rub cut edges with lemon to prevent discoloration.

▶ Arrange artichokes upright in a microwavable dish, in a circle. Space artichokes about 1 inch (2.5 cm) apart. Pour water over and cover with plastic wrap.

▶ Microwave at High (100%) for 6 to 10 minutes, or until tender when the base is pierced with a knife. If necessary, rotate dish partway through cooking. Let stand, covered, for 10 minutes. Drain. Scoop out and discard the hairy choke. Serve with Hollandaise.

Makes 4 servings

TIP   To reheat appetizers such as sausage rolls, small quiches or turnovers, place on a napkin-lined plate (the napkin absorbs moisture, preventing sogginess) and heat at Medium-High (70%) or Medium (50%) just until warm.

3
Stocks and Soups

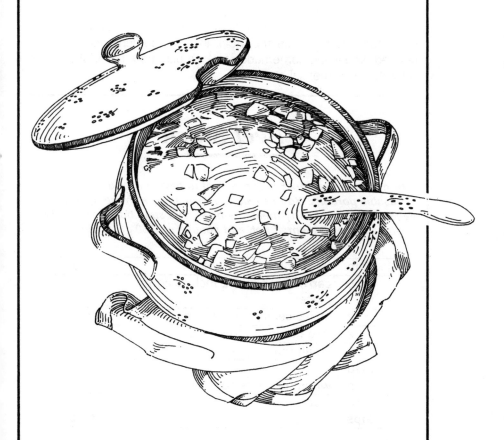

Stocks and soups are traditional comfort foods, usually associated with long simmering on top of the stove. With a microwave oven you can still enjoy homemade soups, though if you make large pots of soup in the microwave, you won't save much time over conventional methods.

Our soup recipes serve from four to six people. Some are hearty meal-in-a-bowl soups that will feed the family on a busy weeknight. Others will make a savory beginning to a special meal, and a few are fresh summer soups that use seasonal produce.

Since microwaving avoids direct heat, soups don't burn easily, and stirring can be almost eliminated. A pretty microwavable casserole or soup tureen can serve as both a cooking and serving dish. Many have lids, which are easier to handle than plastic wrap. The microwave also helps soups keep their fresh flavors and colors, and is especially suited to vegetable and seafood soups, since the ingredients don't become tough and overcooked.

You can also make your own stocks in the microwave, with very little effort. Freeze the stock in small portions and use it as needed; you'll find homemade stocks much more flavorful and less salty than commercial stocks.

Beef Stock

Homemade beef stock is convenient to have on hand. Freeze it in usable portions. You can also serve it as is, with the meat and vegetables, for a hearty meal-in-a-bowl. The soup bones should have some meat on them. If not, add about 8 oz (250 g) stewing beef.

2 lb	beef bones and beef	1 kg
6	carrots, cut into 2 inch (5 cm) pieces	6
2	stalks celery, with leaves	2
2	large onions, quartered	2
1	small bunch parsley	1
1 tsp	salt	5 mL
¼ tsp	whole black peppercorns	1 mL
8 to 10 cups	water	2 to 2.5 L

▶ Spread bones, meat, carrots, celery and onions on a lightly oiled broiler or roasting pan. Broil about 6 inches (15 cm) from element until brown. Turn over and brown other side.

▶ Transfer meat and vegetables from broiler pan to a 16 cup (4 L) microwavable casserole. Add remaining ingredients and enough water to cover. Cover with lid or microwavable dinner plate.

▶ Microwave at High (100%) for 25 to 30 minutes, or until stock comes to a boil.

▶ Skim off any foam. Microwave, covered, at Medium-Low (30%) for 60 to 70 minutes, or until meat and vegetables are tender.

▶ Allow to cool. Strain stock and refrigerate. Remove hardened fat. Store in refrigerator or freeze in usable amounts for other recipes.

Makes about 8 cups (2 L)

Chicken Stock

To make chicken soup, add chopped cooked chicken, chopped vegetables, fine egg noodles or rice. Or freeze the stock in 1 or 2 cup (250 or 500 mL) amounts to be used in other recipes.

2 to 3 lb	stewing or boiling chicken	1 to 1.5 kg
4	carrots	4
6	stalks celery, with leaves	6
1	small bunch parsley	1
2	onions, quartered	2
2 tsp	salt	10 mL
1 tsp	freshly ground black pepper	5 mL
8 cups	water	2 L

▶ Cut up chicken. Cut carrots and celery into 2 inch (5 cm) pieces. Put all ingredients except water in a 16 cup (4 L) microwavable casserole. Add water to cover. (A small microwavable plate can be placed over the ingredients to keep the chicken under the liquid.)

▶ Cover and microwave at High (100%) for 25 to 30 minutes, or until stock comes to a boil.

▶ Skim off any foam. Set the lid ajar and microwave at Medium-Low (30%) for 60 minutes.

▶ Allow to cool. Strain and refrigerate. Remove hardened fat.

▶ Use to make chicken soup or keep in refrigerator or freezer.

Makes about 8 cups (2 L)

Leek, Carrot and Tomato Soup with Garlic Croutons

A colorful vegetable soup that's easy and fast. The croutons can also be used in other soups, or salads.

CROUTONS

¼ cup	butter	50 mL
1	clove garlic, slivered	1
3	slices bread, crusts removed, diced	3

SOUP

2 tbsp	butter	25 mL
3	leeks, white part only, well cleaned and sliced	3
2	carrots, chopped	2
2	stalks celery, chopped	2
1	19 oz (540 mL) can tomatoes, undrained	1
2 cups	chicken stock	500 mL
1 tsp	dried basil	5 mL
½ tsp	dried thyme	2 mL
	Salt and freshly ground black pepper to taste	

▶ To make croutons, melt butter in a large shallow microwavable dish or pie plate at High (100%) for 40 to 60 seconds. Stir in garlic and microwave at High (100%) for 1 minute. Add bread cubes and toss until evenly coated with butter. Microwave, uncovered, at High (100%) for 4 to 5 minutes, stirring every minute, until lightly brown. (Croutons will continue to cook and crisp during standing time.)

▶ To make soup, in an 8 cup (2 L) glass measure or microwavable casserole, combine butter, leeks, carrots and celery. Cover and microwave at High (100%) for 5 to 6 minutes, or until vegetables are softened. Stir once during cooking.

▶ Add tomatoes and their juice, and mash with potato masher. Add chicken stock and seasonings. Cover and microwave at High (100%) for 14 to 16 minutes, or until vegetables are tender. Stir once during cooking. Let stand for 5 to 10 minutes before serving. Garnish each bowl with croutons.

Makes 6 cups (1.5 L)

Chilled Tomato Soup with Dill

This is an excellent soup to prepare when the summer is hot and tomatoes are at their peak.

2 lb	ripe tomatoes (about 6 to 8 medium)	1 kg
1 tbsp	granulated sugar	15 mL
1 tsp	salt	5 mL
1 tbsp	finely chopped onion	15 mL
2 tbsp	lemon juice	25 mL
1 tbsp	grated lemon rind	15 mL
1	cucumber, peeled, seeded and finely diced	1
1 tbsp	chopped fresh dill, or 1 tsp (5 mL) dried dill weed	15 mL
1 cup	whipping cream	250 mL
	Sprigs of fresh dill for garnish, optional	

▶ Halve and seed the tomatoes. Place in an 8 cup (2 L) microwavable casserole, cover and microwave at High (100%) for 10 to 12 minutes, or until soft. Stir partway through cooking. Allow the tomatoes to cool until they can be handled, then slip off the skins.
▶ Puree the tomatoes in a blender or food processor. Add remaining ingredients except the cream. Chill.
▶ Just before serving, stir in the cream. Garnish each serving with a sprig of fresh dill.

Makes about 6 cups (1.5 L)

TIP Dry bread for breadcrumbs or croutons. Spread 2 cups (500 mL) bread cubes in a shallow microwavable dish and microwave, uncovered, at High (100%) for 2 to 4 minutes, or until dry. Stir or shake dish often during cooking.

Seafood Bisque

Use any combination of seafood to make up one pound (500 g). If you are using frozen fish, cut it up without thawing and add 2 to 3 minutes to the cooking time.

2	small leeks	2
2 tbsp	butter	25 mL
1	clove garlic, minced	1
1 cup	sliced mushrooms	250 mL
8 oz	fresh or frozen fish, cut into ½ inch (1 cm) pieces	250 g
4 oz	uncooked peeled shrimp or scallops	125 g
4 oz	shelled crabmeat or lobster	125 g
¼ tsp	salt	1 mL
¼ tsp	freshly ground black pepper	1 mL
pinch	cayenne	pinch
3 cups	chicken stock	750 mL
½ cup	soft breadcrumbs	125 mL
½ cup	cream	125 mL
2 tbsp	white vermouth	25 mL

▶ Cut leeks in half lengthwise and wash well under cold running water. Slice thinly, including about 1 inch (2.5 cm) of the green.
▶ Combine butter, leeks and garlic in an 8 cup (2 L) glass measure or microwavable casserole. Microwave, uncovered, at High (100%) for 2 minutes.
▶ Stir in mushrooms and microwave, uncovered, at High (100%) for 2 to 4 minutes, or until vegetables are tender.
▶ Add fish, shellfish, seasonings and chicken stock. Cover and microwave at High (100%) for 10 to 14 minutes, stirring partway through, until fish is opaque and flakes easily with a fork.
▶ Add breadcrumbs and cream and microwave at High (100%) for 1 to 2 minutes, or until hot. Stir in vermouth and serve.

Makes 6 cups (1.5 L)

Boston Clam Chowder

A traditional recipe that can be a light meal when served with crusty bread. If you are using tender, red-skinned potatoes, leave the skin on for texture and color.

4	slices bacon, diced	4
1	onion, chopped	1
2	large potatoes, cubed	2
¼ cup	chopped green pepper	50 mL
¼ cup	chopped red pepper	50 mL
1	5½ oz (142 g) can clams, undrained	1
½ tsp	salt	2 mL
¼ tsp	freshly ground black pepper	1 mL
¼ tsp	dried thyme	1 mL
2 cups	milk, or part cream and part milk	500 mL

▶ In an 8 cup (2 L) microwavable casserole, cover bacon with paper towel. Microwave at Medium-High (70%) for 3 to 4 minutes, or until almost crisp. Stir partway through cooking to separate the pieces.

▶ Add the onion and potatoes. Cover and microwave at High (100%) for 8 to 10 minutes, or until potatoes are tender. Stir partway through cooking.

▶ Remove a few spoonfuls of potato, mash them and return to casserole.

▶ Add the remaining ingredients and microwave at High (100%) for 3 to 4 minutes, or until soup is hot but not boiling.

Makes about 4 cups (1 L)

TIP To separate cold bacon slices more easily, unwrap package and microwave at High (100%) for 30 to 60 seconds.

Creole Cod Chowder

A hearty soup with lots of flavor and "heat." Serve it with crusty bread and a green salad. If you are using frozen fish, cut it into pieces without thawing and add 2 to 3 minutes to the cooking time.

1 tbsp	vegetable oil	15 mL
2	stalks celery, chopped	2
1	small green pepper, chopped	1
1	onion, chopped	1
2	cloves garlic, minced	2
1	28 oz (796 mL) can tomatoes, undrained	1
1 cup	fish or chicken stock	250 mL
½ tsp	salt	2 mL
½ tsp	dried thyme	2 mL
½ tsp	dried oregano	2 mL
¼ tsp	freshly ground black pepper	1 mL
¼ tsp	cayenne	1 mL
1 tsp	Worcestershire sauce	5 mL
dash	Tabasco	dash
1 lb	cod or other firm-fleshed fish, fresh or frozen, cut into 1 inch (2.5 cm) pieces	500 g

▶ In a 12 cup (3 L) microwavable casserole, heat oil for 1 minute. Stir in celery, green pepper, onion and garlic and microwave, uncovered, at High (100%) for 4 to 5 minutes, or until vegetables are soft. Stir partway through cooking time.
▶ Add tomatoes with their juice and mash with a potato masher. Add stock and all seasonings. Cover with vented plastic wrap or casserole lid and microwave at High (100%) for 5 to 6 minutes, or until mixture comes to a boil.
▶ Add fish, cover and microwave at High (100%) for 7 to 9 minutes, until fish is opaque. Stir partway through cooking time. Let stand for 5 minutes before serving.

Makes 8 cups (2 L)

Double Mushroom Soup with Blue Cheese

A creamy mushroom soup with the subtle flavor of blue cheese. The dried mushrooms add a richness to the mushroom flavor. Because they are rehydrated during cooking, you do not need to soak them first.

2 tbsp	butter	25 mL
1½ cups	sliced fresh mushrooms	375 mL
1	onion, chopped	1
¼ cup	all-purpose flour	50 mL
½ tsp	salt	2 mL
¼ tsp	freshly ground black pepper	1 mL
3 cups	chicken stock	750 mL
¼ cup	dried mushrooms, rinsed	50 mL
½ cup	cream	125 mL
¼ cup	crumbled blue cheese	50 mL

▶ In an 8 cup (2 L) glass measure or microwavable casserole, combine butter, sliced mushrooms and onions. Microwave, uncovered, at High (100%) for 2 to 3 minutes, or until vegetables are softened.
▶ Blend in flour, salt and pepper and microwave, uncovered, at High (100%) for 30 seconds.
▶ Stir in chicken stock and dried mushrooms. Cover and microwave at High (100%) for 10 to 14 minutes, or until mixture comes to boil and thickens. Stir partway through cooking. Stir in cream and top with crumbled cheese. Serve immediately.

Makes 5 cups (1.25 L)

TIP Warm rolls or small loaves of bread on a microwave roasting rack to prevent sogginess. Avoid overheating, or bread will harden. Microwave at Medium (50%) for 1 to 1½ minutes, or until barely warm.

Red Pepper Soup

This soup is a beautiful color and is good served either hot or cold. The gin gives it a nice kick.

2 tbsp	butter	25 mL
3	large red peppers, about 1 lb (500 g), cored and cut into chunks	3
2 tbsp	all-purpose flour	25 mL
1 tbsp	paprika	15 mL
½ tsp	salt	2 mL
¼ tsp	freshly ground black pepper	1 mL
3 cups	chicken stock	750 mL
2 tbsp	gin	25 mL
¼ cup	plain yogurt	50 mL

▶ Combine butter and peppers in an 8 cup (2 L) glass measure or microwavable casserole. Cover and microwave at High (100%) for 6 to 8 minutes, stirring occasionally, until peppers are tender.
▶ Stir in flour, paprika, salt and pepper until well blended. Microwave, uncovered, at High (100%) for 1 minute.
▶ Gradually whisk in chicken stock until smooth. Cover and microwave at High (100%) for 6 to 8 minutes, or until soup comes to a boil and thickens slightly. Stir occasionally.
▶ Puree mixture in batches in food processor or blender until smooth. Add gin and, if serving hot, taste and adjust seasonings. Garnish each serving with a spoonful of yogurt.
▶ If serving cold, cover and chill until ready to serve. Then taste and adjust seasonings. (Soup may need different amounts of salt and pepper when cold.) Top each bowl with a spoonful of yogurt.

Makes 4 cups (1 L)

Cajun Corn Chowder

When fresh corn and tomatoes are both in season, this is the soup to make!

2 tbsp	butter	25 mL
1	onion, chopped	1
1	red pepper, chopped	1
2 cups	fresh or frozen corn kernels (about 3 ears)	500 mL
1	tomato, seeded and chopped	1
1 cup	chicken stock	250 mL
½ tsp	salt	2 mL
¼ tsp	freshly ground black pepper	1 mL
¼ to ½ tsp	hot red pepper flakes	1 to 2 mL
1 cup	milk	250 mL

▶ In an 8 cup (2 L) glass measure or microwavable casserole, combine butter, onion and red pepper. Microwave, uncovered, at High (100%) for 3 to 4 minutes, or until vegetables are softened.

▶ Add corn, tomato, chicken stock and seasonings. Cover and microwave at High (100%) for 14 to 16 minutes, or until corn is tender.

▶ Stir in milk and process in batches in food processor until almost smooth. Return to dish and microwave, covered, until hot but not boiling, about 1 to 2 minutes at High (100%).

Makes about 5 cups (1.25 L)

TIP To prevent boilovers when making sauces, cereals or soups, use a large glass measure and fill only half full. The handle stays cool and makes the cup easy to hold when stirring.

Green Pea and Potato Soup

A bright-green soup that is good hot or cold. The potato provides thickening.

2 tbsp	butter	25 mL
1	onion, chopped	1
2	potatoes, peeled and chopped, about 8 oz (250 g)	2
1	10 oz (350 g) package frozen peas	1
2½ cups	milk	625 mL
1 tsp	salt	5 mL
1 tsp	granulated sugar	5 mL
¼ tsp	freshly ground white pepper	1 mL
pinch	cayenne	pinch

▶ Combine butter, onion and potatoes in an 8 cup (2 L) glass measure or microwavable casserole. Cover and microwave at High (100%) for 5 to 6 minutes, or until potatoes are almost tender. Stir partway through cooking.

▶ Add frozen peas, cover and microwave at High (100%) for 5 to 6 minutes, or until peas are tender. Stir partway through cooking.

▶ Stir in remaining ingredients, cover and microwave at High (100%) for 4 to 6 minutes, or until hot. Stir partway through cooking.

▶ Process in batches in food processor or blender until smooth. Reheat if necessary and taste and adjust seasonings before serving.

Makes 5 cups (1.25 L)

4
Meat

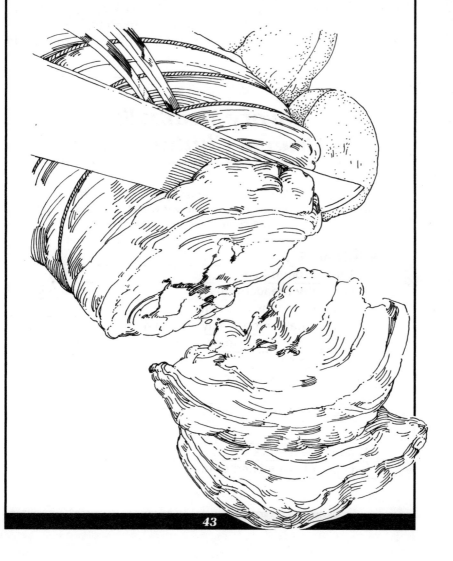

Microwaving meat can produce juicy, tender new specialties. Meats should, however, be watched carefully in the microwave, and should not be overcooked. Although we find that less tender cuts such as beef shanks or stewing meats need the slow-cooking of conventional methods, medium-tender or tender cuts develop flavor without toughening when cooked at lower power levels in the microwave. Ground meats can usually be microwaved at High (100%) but use Medium (50%) for cuts such as round, sirloin tip or beef tenderloin.

Choose evenly shaped boneless roasts, and chops of equal thickness. Cut meat pieces the same size and shape so they will cook at the same rate.

A microwave roasting rack and microwave thermometer are useful accessories. Roasts are elevated on a rack to prevent them from steaming in their own juices, and a thermometer or temperature probe will provide accuracy when determining internal temperature.

Savory Meatballs in Orange Chutney Sauce

This delicious dish doubles as either an appetizer—just keep warm in a chafing dish or fondue pot and skewer with toothpicks—or as a main course served over noodles or rice.

MEATBALLS

1 lb	ground beef	500 g
½ cup	dry breadcrumbs	125 mL
1	egg, lightly beaten	1
1	small onion, finely chopped	1
1	clove garlic, minced	1
1 tsp	horseradish	5 mL
1 tsp	Worcestershire sauce	5 mL
½ tsp	salt	2 mL
¼ tsp	freshly ground black pepper	1 mL

SAUCE

¾ cup	beef stock	175 mL
¾ cup	unsweetened orange juice	175 mL

⅓ cup	chutney	75 mL
4 tsp	cornstarch	20 mL
2 tbsp	soy sauce	25 mL
2 tsp	Dijon mustard	10 mL
1 tsp	horseradish	5 mL

▶ To make meatballs, combine beef, breadcrumbs, egg, onion, garlic, horseradish, Worcestershire, salt and pepper. Mix well and shape into 1 inch (2.5 cm) balls.

▶ Arrange meatballs evenly on a microwave roasting rack about ½ inch (1 cm) apart. Cover with waxed paper and microwave at High (100%) for 5 to 7 minutes, or until no longer pink. Rearrange meatballs, if necessary, partway through for even cooking. Transfer to a 6 cup (1.5 L) casserole.

▶ In a 4 cup (1 L) glass measure, combine beef stock, orange juice and chutney. Stir cornstarch and soy sauce together and then stir into orange juice mixture to blend. Microwave, uncovered, at High (100%) for 3 to 4 minutes, or until mixture comes to a boil and thickens, stirring partway through. Whisk in mustard and horseradish. Pour over meatballs.

▶ Cover with lid or vented plastic wrap and microwave at High (100%) for 3 to 5 minutes, or until heated through.

Makes about 30 meatballs, or 4 main-course servings

TIP Cook ground meat in a microwavable plastic colander set in a microwavable dish for easy draining of excess fat. One pound (500 g) ground meat should be cooked at High (100%) for 4 to 6 minutes or until no longer pink. Stir often to keep crumbly.

Beef Saos

The lime juice marinade tenderizes and provides flavor. Add more chilies if you wish. Serve over uncooked greens such as spinach, lettuce or bok choy, which will wilt beautifully on warmed plates and under the sauce.

1 lb	boneless round or sirloin tip, thinly sliced	500 g
	Juice of 2 limes	
1	clove garlic, minced	1
1 tsp	grated fresh ginger	5 mL
¼ cup	soy sauce	50 mL
2 tbsp	vegetable oil	25 mL
2	shallots, or 1 small onion, diced	2
1 tbsp	chopped fresh hot chilies	15 mL
1 tbsp	brown sugar	15 mL
⅓ cup	unsalted blanched peanuts	75 mL
2 cups	shredded spinach, lettuce or bok choy	500 mL

▶ In a bowl just large enough to hold the meat, combine the beef, lime juice, garlic, ginger, soy sauce and oil. Toss well. Cover and marinate in refrigerator for 4 hours or overnight.

▶ In an 8 cup (2 L) microwavable casserole, microwave meat and marinade, covered, at Medium (50%) for 8 to 10 minutes, or until beef is brown on the edges but still pink inside. Stir twice during cooking. Remove meat to a warm platter using a slotted spoon.

▶ Add shallots, chilies and brown sugar to liquid in dish. Microwave at High (100%) for 3 minutes. Return meat and combine.

▶ Serve on a bed of shredded greens with the sauce. Garnish with peanuts.

Makes 4 servings

Spinach and Swiss Cheese Meatloaf

*Ring-shaped meatloaves cook evenly and quickly in the microwave. This meatloaf has a spinach covering and a Swiss cheese center, although it can also be made without the spinach.
If you don't have a microwavable ring mold, place a small custard cup or juice glass in the center of a round 6 cup (1.5 L) microwavable baking dish or casserole.*

1½ lb	lean ground beef	750 g
1	onion, chopped	1
1	clove garlic, minced	1
1	egg, lightly beaten	1
2 tbsp	milk	25 mL
¼ cup	dry breadcrumbs	50 mL
2 tsp	horseradish	10 mL
1 tsp	salt	5 mL
½ tsp	freshly ground black pepper	2 mL
½ tsp	dry mustard	2 mL
½ tsp	dried basil	2 mL
½ tsp	dried thyme	2 mL
6 to 8	fresh spinach leaves, washed and dried	6 to 8
1½ cups	grated Swiss cheese	375 mL

▶ Combine ground beef, onion, garlic, egg, milk, breadcrumbs, horseradish and seasonings.
▶ Arrange spinach leaves, stem side up, in a 6 cup (1.5 L) microwavable ring mold. Overlap the leaves to cover the bottom of mold.
▶ Place half the meat mixture over the spinach leaves, being careful not to disturb the leaves. Arrange grated cheese evenly over meat, then top with remaining meat. Pat down.
▶ Cover with waxed paper and microwave at Medium-High (70%) for 12 to 16 minutes, or until internal temperature is 145 to 150 F (62 to 65 C). Rotate dish partway through cooking, if necessary.
▶ Let stand for 10 minutes, then drain off excess liquid and turn out onto a serving platter.

Makes 6 servings

Beef in Garlic and Black Bean Sauce

This dish is wonderfully fragrant and flavorful. Serve it with cooked rice. The salty, pungent fermented Chinese black beans should be lightly rinsed before using.

2 tbsp	rice wine or dry sherry	25 mL
1 tbsp	soy sauce	15 mL
2 tsp	sesame oil	10 mL
1 lb	boneless round or sirloin tip, cut into thin strips	500 g
½ cup	beef stock	125 mL
1 tbsp	cornstarch	15 mL
1 tsp	soy sauce	5 mL
½ tsp	granulated sugar	2 mL
2 tbsp	vegetable oil	25 mL
2	cloves garlic, minced	2
6	green onions, sliced	6
2 tsp	grated fresh ginger	10 mL
2 tbsp	black beans, rinsed and lightly mashed with a fork	25 mL

▶ In a bowl just large enough to hold the beef, combine the rice wine, 1 tbsp (15 mL) soy sauce and sesame oil. Toss beef in mixture and marinate for 30 minutes at room temperature. (If marinated any longer, cover and refrigerate.)

▶ Meanwhile, in a cup or small bowl, combine the stock, cornstarch, 1 tsp (5 mL) soy sauce and sugar. Set aside.

▶ In a heavy glass 8 cup (2 L) microwavable casserole, microwave vegetable oil at High (100%) for 2 minutes. Add garlic, green onions, ginger and black beans. Microwave, uncovered, at High (100%) for 1 minute.

▶ Add beef and marinade. Cover and microwave at Medium (50%) for 2 minutes.

▶ Stir in stock mixture. Cover and microwave at Medium (50%) for 4 to 6 minutes, or until the sauce has thickened slightly. Do not overcook the beef—it should still be slightly rare. Stir once during cooking.

Makes 4 servings

Filet of Beef in Black Peppercorn Crust

A dish fit for a king, but easy enough for the novice. Crush the peppercorns with a mortar and pestle or a rolling pin.
Make sure the filet is even in shape. Use about 1 inch (2.5 cm) per person and adjust the cooking time accordingly.

1½ lb	beef filet (beef tenderloin)	750 g
1 tbsp	butter, softened	15 mL
¼ cup	coarsely crushed black peppercorns	50 mL
2 tbsp	butter	25 mL
6	shallots, chopped	6
¼ cup	cream	50 mL
¼ cup	brandy	50 mL

▶ Rub the meat completely with the softened butter, and roll in crushed peppercorns. Press any leftover peppercorns into meat.

▶ Place meat in a shallow glass dish that is slightly larger than the filet. Shield the ends of the filet with small pieces of foil.

▶ Microwave, uncovered, at Medium-High (70%) for 18 to 20 minutes for rare and 20 to 22 minutes for medium. Remove the foil halfway through the cooking time. Transfer meat to a warm platter.

▶ Add 2 tbsp (25 mL) butter to the cooking dish along with the shallots. Microwave, uncovered, at High (100%) for 3 to 5 minutes, or until shallots are softened. Stir to incorporate the meat drippings and shallots. Add the cream and microwave, uncovered, at High (100%) for 1 to 2 minutes, or until hot.

▶ Add brandy and ignite with a match. The heat from the dish should be enough to ignite the brandy.

▶ To serve, slice the filet into 6 pieces and place on individual warm plates. Pour sauce over each serving.

Makes 6 servings

Mushroom-filled Veal Patties with Gorgonzola

A juicy, delectable main course, quickly prepared and cooked. Serve with fettuccine and green beans.

1 lb	ground veal	500 g
½ cup	dry breadcrumbs	125 mL
1 tbsp	brandy, optional	15 mL
½ tsp	salt	2 mL
¼ tsp	freshly ground black pepper	1 mL
¼ tsp	ground sage	1 mL
1	egg, lightly beaten	1
6	mushrooms, chopped	6
2 tbsp	soy sauce	25 mL
3 oz	Gorgonzola cheese	90 g
2 tbsp	chopped parsley	25 mL

▶ Combine veal, breadcrumbs, brandy, seasonings and egg. Form mixture into eight thin patties. Divide chopped mushrooms among four patties. Top these with remaining patties. Seal the edges by pinching together.

▶ Place patties in a shallow microwavable dish. Brush with soy sauce. Cover with waxed paper and microwave at Medium-High (70%) for 7 to 10 minutes, or until no longer pink. Turn patties over and rearrange halfway through cooking time and brush with soy sauce.

▶ Top each patty with an equal amount of cheese. Cover and microwave at High (100%) for 30 to 40 seconds, or until cheese is melted. Let stand for 5 minutes. Garnish with chopped parsley.

Makes 4 servings

Veal with Oyster Mushrooms and Ground Hazelnuts

A delicious combination that is both easy and elegant. Serve with rice pilaf or fettuccine and a crisp green salad.

4	veal scallops, about 12 oz (375 g)	4
8	oyster mushrooms	8
2 tbsp	chopped parsley	25 mL
pinch	ground nutmeg	pinch
pinch	freshly ground black pepper	pinch
¼ cup	butter	50 mL
½ cup	ground hazelnuts	125 mL
1 tsp	dried rosemary	5 mL
4	sprigs parsley for garnish	4

▶ Pound veal scallops thin with a mallet. Chop 4 of the mushrooms coarsely. Put one-quarter of the chopped mushrooms and parsley on each piece of veal. Sprinkle with nutmeg and pepper. Roll up.

▶ Melt the butter in a small shallow dish at High (100%) for 30 to 40 seconds. Put the ground hazelnuts and rosemary in another shallow dish.

▶ Dip the veal rolls in the butter and then in the nuts, coating evenly. This should use up all the nuts and butter. If not, sprinkle or pat remaining nuts on the top and pour on the butter.

▶ Place veal rolls in round 8 inch (20 cm) microwavable dish. Cover with vented plastic wrap or lid. Microwave at Medium (50%) for 8 to 10 minutes, or until veal is no longer pink. Rotate dish during cooking if necessary.

▶ Spoon the sauce that has accumulated over the meat. Add the remaining mushrooms to the dish. Cover and microwave at High (100%) for 1 minute.

▶ Serve each roll with some of the sauce, a mushroom and a sprig of parsley for garnish.

Makes 4 servings

Boneless Leg of Lamb Stuffed with Pesto

The garlicky flavor of pesto produces just the right mouth-watering aroma, as well as complementing the delicate flavor of the lamb. When sliced, the pinwheel of meat and green filling requires no garnish.

1	3 lb (1.5 kg) boneless leg of lamb	1
⅓ cup	pesto sauce	75 mL
1 tbsp	white wine	15 mL
1 tbsp	soy sauce	15 mL
1 tbsp	olive oil	15 mL

▶ Make pesto sauce (see below).

▶ If the meat does not open out flat, cut through the thicker flesh so it will roll up evenly.

▶ Spread meat with pesto sauce. Roll the meat into its former shape, and tie it several times with string. Place in a shallow microwavable dish.

▶ Combine wine, soy sauce and olive oil. Brush over meat, and pour remainder in bottom of dish.

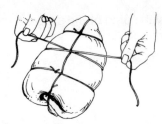

▶ Cover lamb with waxed or parchment paper, tucking the paper close to the meat. This will keep the meat from drying out.
▶ Microwave at Medium (50%) for 10 minutes. Turn meat over and baste. Microwave at Medium-Low (30%) for 4 to 7 minutes per pound (500 g), or until internal temperature reaches 140 F (60 C) for medium. Use a regular meat thermometer outside of the microwave if you do not have a microwave thermometer. Partway through cooking time, turn meat over and baste.
▶ Let stand, covered, for 15 minutes before carving. Slice and serve. Remove string after slicing.
▶ Warm the basting sauce at High (100%) for 1 minute and spoon onto each serving.

Makes 6 servings

Pesto Sauce

When basil is plentiful, make batches of this recipe and freeze in small containers. Serve the sauce on pasta with an extra grating of cheese. If fresh basil is not available, substitute the same amount of flat-leaf Italian parsley plus 2 tbsp (25 mL) dried basil. If you are making the pesto to freeze, make it without the cheese, and stir in the Parmesan when the sauce is completely defrosted.

2 cups	fresh basil leaves, packed	500 mL
1 tsp	salt	5 mL
½ tsp	freshly ground black pepper	2 mL
2	cloves garlic	2
¼ cup	pine nuts	50 mL
1 cup	olive oil	250 mL
½ cup	grated Parmesan cheese	125 mL

▶ Place basil, salt, pepper, garlic, pine nuts and oil in blender or food processor. Process until smooth. Stir in cheese.

Makes 2 cups (500 mL)

TIP To freshen the microwave oven of food odors, combine 1 cup (125 mL) water and ½ lemon in a 2 cup (500 mL) glass measure. Microwave at High (100%) for 5 minutes.

Sweetbreads in Porcini and Port Sauce

Sweetbreads are a delicacy, though they are not always easy to find. This dish requires a bit of preparation, but it is worth the trouble, as the sweetbreads are very tender and delicious prepared this way.

1 lb	veal sweetbreads	500 g
1 cup	water	250 mL
1 tbsp	lemon juice	15 mL
¼ cup	dried porcini mushrooms	50 mL
2 tbsp	butter	25 mL
1	onion, chopped	1
1 cup	sliced fresh mushrooms	250 mL
2 tbsp	all-purpose flour	25 mL
½ tsp	salt	2 mL
¼ tsp	freshly ground black pepper	1 mL
½ cup	chicken stock	125 mL
¼ cup	port	50 mL
¼ cup	whipping cream	50 mL

▶ Soak sweetbreads in several changes of cold water to remove excess blood. When water remains clear, pierce them lightly in several places and place in an 8 cup (2 L) microwavable casserole. Add water and lemon juice.

▶ Cover and microwave at High (100%) for 6 to 8 minutes, or until sweetbreads are firm, light in color and tender. Stir gently partway through cooking. Let stand, covered, for 5 minutes.

▶ Meanwhile, crumble dried mushrooms in a small bowl and cover with warm water.

▶ Drain cooking liquid off sweetbreads and cover with cold water. With fingers, remove membrane, fat and tubes attached to membrane. Slice sweetbreads in ½ inch (1 cm) slices and set aside.

▶ Drain dried mushrooms.

▶ In same 8 cup (2 L) casserole, combine butter and onion. Microwave, uncovered, at High (100%) for 1 minute. Add dried and fresh mushrooms and microwave, uncovered, at High (100%) for 2 to 3 minutes, or until mushrooms are softened.

▶ Stir in flour, salt and pepper. Microwave, uncovered, at High

(100%) for 30 seconds. Gradually whisk in chicken stock until smooth.
▶ Cover and microwave at High (100%) for 2 to 3 minutes, or until mixture comes to a boil and thickens. Stir partway through cooking time.
▶ Stir in port and cream until smooth. Gently stir in sweetbreads. Cover and microwave at Medium-High (70%) for 2 to 3 minutes, or until hot. Serve over cooked noodles.

Makes 4 main-course servings, or 6 appetizer servings

Glazed Peameal Bacon

This is an easy roast to serve at a family meal or as part of a brunch buffet.

1 lb	piece peameal bacon	500 g
¼ cup	dark beer or stout	50 mL
¼ cup	Hot and Sweet Mustard (page 183) or German-style mustard	50 mL

▶ Rinse cornmeal from bacon and place in a shallow microwavable dish. Pour on beer. Cover with waxed paper and microwave at Medium (50%) for 15 minutes.
▶ Stir mustard into drippings. Glaze bacon with drippings. Turn over and microwave at Medium (50%) for 8 to 12 minutes, or until internal temperature reaches 160 F (70 C). Slice to serve.

Makes 4 servings

TIP To warm up a plate of food for a late diner, prepare a dinner plate, arranging longer-cooking or denser foods to outer edges, quicker-heating items in the center. Cover with waxed paper or plastic wrap and refrigerate. Reheat at Medium-High (70%) for 2 to 3 minutes, or until warmed through.

Orange Ginger Pork
with Rice

A delicious way to use leftover pork—or beef, turkey or chicken for that matter. Serve with a green vegetable or salad, and you've got a delicious meal that's faster than fast food.

1	orange	1
2 tbsp	butter	25 mL
1	onion, chopped	1
1 cup	long-grain rice	250 mL
2 to 3 cups	cubed cooked pork	500 to 750 mL
1½ cups	chicken stock	375 mL
½ cup	orange juice	125 mL
½ cup	slivered almonds	125 mL
¼ cup	raisins	50 mL
1 tbsp	grated fresh ginger	15 mL
1 tsp	ground cumin	5 mL
¼ tsp	salt	1 mL
¼ tsp	freshly ground black pepper	1 mL

▶ Grate rind of orange. With a sharp knife, remove remaining pith from orange and slice orange in crosswise slices. Reserve.
▶ Combine butter, onion and rice in an 8 cup (2 L) microwavable casserole. Microwave, uncovered, at High (100%) for 2 to 3 minutes, or until onion is soft. Stir partway through cooking time.
▶ Stir in orange rind and all remaining ingredients except orange slices. Cover and microwave at High (100%) for 15 to 20 minutes, or until liquid is absorbed and rice is tender. Stir once or twice during cooking.
▶ Arrange orange slices on top of casserole and let stand for 10 minutes before serving.

Makes 4 to 6 servings

Szechuan Pork
with Peanuts

A hot and spicy recipe, but not as oily as most Szechuan dishes. One hot pepper may be enough for timid types, while four peppers are de rigueur for braver souls. Any kind of hot peppers can be used, but red chilies will add color.
Serve this with rice or noodles to quell the fire.

2 tbsp	peanut oil	25 mL
1	clove garlic, minced	1
1 lb	boneless lean pork, cut into ½ inch (1 cm) strips	500 g
1 to 4	chilies or other hot peppers, chopped	1 to 4
2 tsp	grated fresh ginger	10 mL
6	green onions, sliced	6
1 tbsp	cornstarch	15 mL
1 tbsp	rice wine	15 mL
2 tbsp	soy sauce	25 mL
2 tsp	rice or white vinegar	10 mL
2 tsp	granulated sugar	10 mL
½ tsp	salt	2 mL
½ cup	unsalted blanched peanuts	125 mL

▶ In a heavy 8 cup (2 L) casserole, heat oil, uncovered, at High (100%) for 2 minutes. Stir in garlic and pork. Cover with lid or waxed paper and microwave at Medium (50%) for 5 minutes, stirring twice during cooking.
▶ Add the chilies, ginger and green onions.
▶ In a small bowl or cup, combine the remaining ingredients except the peanuts and stir into the pork mixture. Cover and microwave at Medium (50%) for 7 to 9 minutes, or until the pork has lost its pink color.
▶ Stir in peanuts and serve.

Makes 4 servings

Pork Medallions
in Roquefort Cream Sauce

A delicious sauce with a mild blue cheese flavor. Serve over cooked noodles or rice.

2 tbsp	vegetable oil	25 mL
1½ lb	pork tenderloin, cut into ½ inch (1 cm) slices	750 g
2 tbsp	butter	25 mL
1	onion, chopped	1
1 cup	sliced mushrooms	250 mL
2 tbsp	all-purpose flour	25 mL
½ tsp	salt	2 mL
½ tsp	ground cumin	2 mL
¼ tsp	freshly ground black pepper	1 mL
½ cup	dry vermouth or white wine	125 mL
½ cup	chicken stock	125 mL
¼ cup	crumbled Roquefort or blue cheese	50 mL
½ cup	plain yogurt or sour cream	125 mL

▶ Heat oil in a large skillet on stove top. Quickly sauté pork slices on both sides, until just lightly browned. Remove with slotted spoon and set aside. Cook in batches, if necessary.

▶ In an 8 cup (2 L) microwavable casserole, combine butter, onion and mushrooms. Microwave, uncovered, at High (100%) for 2 to 3 minutes, or until softened.

▶ Stir in flour, salt, cumin and pepper and microwave at High (100%) for 1 minute. Whisk in vermouth and chicken stock. Cover and microwave at High (100%) for 2 to 3 minutes, or until sauce boils.

▶ Stir in pork slices, cover and microwave at High (100%) for 5 minutes. Stir, cover and microwave at Medium (50%) for 10 to 15 minutes, or until pork is tender and no longer pink in the center.

▶ Stir in cheese, mashing to blend with hot sauce. Stir in yogurt or sour cream. Microwave at Medium-High (70%) for 2 to 3 minutes, or just until heated through. Do not boil.

Makes 6 servings

Chinese Roast Pork

Hot or cold, this roast is moist and delicious. To serve it cold, slice thinly and serve with Hot and Sweet Mustard (page 183) or a hot pepper relish. This dish is a terrific make-ahead item for a buffet table. The round, compact shape of the roast makes it perfect for cooking in the microwave.

2 tbsp	hoisin sauce	25 mL
2 tbsp	soy sauce	25 mL
1 tbsp	rice wine	15 mL
1 tbsp	honey	15 mL
1 tsp	sesame oil	5 mL
1 tsp	grated fresh ginger	5 mL
½ tsp	five spice powder	2 mL
1½ lb	center cut boneless pork loin roast, about 3 to 4 inches (8 to 10 cm) in diameter	750 g

▶ Combine all ingredients except for roast and pour into a leakproof plastic bag. Add roast, seal and marinate overnight in refrigerator. Turn roast occasionally to coat with marinade.

▶ To cook, remove from marinade and place on a microwave roasting rack. Cover with waxed paper and microwave at High (100%) for 5 minutes. Turn roast over. (If you are using a microwave temperature probe, insert it horizontally into the roast at this point.) Reduce power level to Medium (50%) and continue cooking for 15 to 20 minutes, or until the internal temperature is 160 to 165 F (70 to 72 C).

▶ Loosely cover roast with foil and let stand for 10 minutes. The internal temperature should increase to 170 F (75 C) during standing time. Slice thinly. Serve hot or cold.

Makes 6 servings

TIP   Microwave roasting racks are now available in all shapes and sizes. They are good for elevating roasts, cooking bacon, reheating appetizers and sandwiches. Buy the largest one that will fit in your microwave oven. If you do not have a roasting rack, substitute an inverted microwavable saucer on a plate and balance the food on the saucer.

5
Poultry

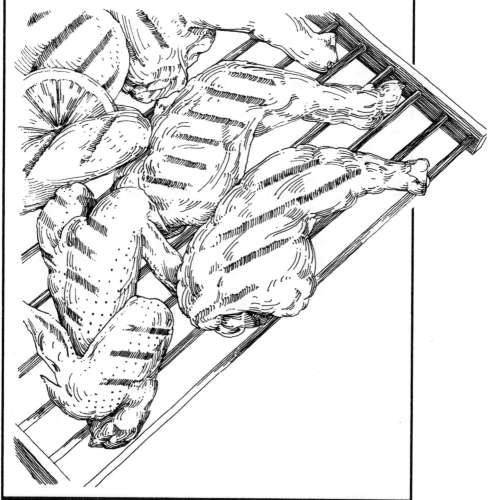

Poultry is ideal for microwave cooking. It also cooks quickly, which makes it perfect for fast, easy meals. We particularly like teaming the microwave with the broiler or barbecue. Precooking in the microwave for 4 minutes per pound (500 g) before grilling combines the best of both worlds—speed and moistness, with the flavor and crispness of the barbecue.

Poultry parts, particularly breasts, can often be purchased boned and/or skinned. Check the recipe ingredient list to determine whether the poultry is weighed with bone and skin or not. The cooking time for poultry is calculated at 6 to 8 minutes per pound (500 g) at High (100%). If you remove the skin and/or bones, you reduce the weight and should therefore reduce the cooking time accordingly.

Poultry Tips

▶ To ensure even cooking, completely defrost the poultry before cooking.
▶ The arrangement of chicken pieces is important for even cooking. Arrange in a single layer with the thicker, meatier portions toward the outer edges of a shallow dish. It may be necessary to rearrange the pieces partway through the cooking time, depending on the cooking pattern of your microwave oven.
▶ Pierce the skin in several places with a small knife or skewer to prevent the skin from popping or bursting.
▶ If you are concerned about fat and calories, remove the skin before cooking. Baste the poultry for additional flavor and color.
▶ Whether to cover or not depends on the recipe. Cover with waxed paper to hold in splattering without steaming. Cover with vented plastic wrap or a lid when steaming or poaching. For crumb-coated parts or when roasting a whole chicken, microwave uncovered.
▶ When roasting a whole chicken or parts with a crumb coating, use a microwave roasting rack. This helps to prevent the food from steaming in the pan juices and keeps them as crisp as possible.
▶ To test for doneness, pierce cooked poultry at its thickest part. The meat should feel tender, and the juices should run clear, not pink, when pierced.
▶ Standing time, whether for a whole chicken or poultry parts, is necessary to complete the cooking. Cover whole birds loosely with foil and let stand for 10 to 15 minutes. Cover parts and let stand for 5 to 10 minutes.

Chicken Breasts in Creamy Mushroom Sauce

Chicken breasts poached in the microwave are very tender and moist. If you prefer, you can debone and skin the chicken breasts first, but adjust the cooking time accordingly. The mushroom cream sauce is easy enough for everyday eating, but special enough for guests, too.

1 cup	sliced mushrooms	250 mL
3	green onions, sliced	3
2 tbsp	all-purpose flour	25 mL
¼ tsp	salt	1 mL
¼ tsp	freshly ground black pepper	1 mL
¼ tsp	curry powder	1 mL
¼ tsp	paprika	1 mL
4	single chicken breasts, about 8 oz (250 g) each	4
¼ cup	dry white wine	50 mL
½ cup	grated white Cheddar or Swiss cheese	125 mL
¼ cup	light cream	50 mL

▶ Sprinkle mushrooms and green onions in the bottom of a shallow microwavable dish that will hold the chicken breasts in one layer.

▶ Combine flour and seasonings in a plastic bag. Toss chicken breasts in flour mixture. Arrange chicken breasts over the mushrooms, skin side up and with the meatiest portions toward the outer edges of dish. Sprinkle with any remaining seasoned flour.

▶ Pour wine over chicken. Cover with waxed paper and microwave at High (100%) for 12 to 16 minutes—6 to 8 minutes per pound (500 g)—or until chicken is tender and juices run clear when the meat is pierced.

▶ Remove chicken to a serving platter and cover to keep warm.

▶ Stir cheese into cooking liquid. Stir in cream and microwave, uncovered, at Medium (50%) for 2 to 3 minutes, or until cheese melts completely and sauce thickens slightly. Stir and pour over chicken. Serve immediately.

Makes 4 servings

Spicy Roast Chicken

A favorite recipe often used to demonstrate the technique of roasting a whole chicken in the microwave. It has good color, moistness and a wonderful aroma and flavor.

3 to 4 lb	roasting chicken	1.5 to 2 kg
¼ cup	butter	50 mL
2 tsp	curry powder	10 mL
1 tsp	dried tarragon	5 mL
1 tsp	Worcestershire sauce	5 mL
½ tsp	dry mustard	2 mL
¼ tsp	paprika	1 mL
1	clove garlic, minced	1

▶ Clean chicken. Tie wings and legs close to body to make a compact shape. Pierce skin in several places. Place chicken breast side down on a microwave roasting rack.

▶ Melt butter in small microwavable bowl at High (100%) for 40 to 60 seconds. Stir in remaining ingredients. Baste chicken with sauce.
▶ Microwave, uncovered, at High (100%) for 6 to 8 minutes per pound (500 g), turning chicken over partway through cooking time. Chicken is done when juices run clear when pierced. Wrap entire chicken loosely in aluminum foil and let stand for 10 to 15 minutes before carving. During this time the chicken will continue to cook through to the center.

Makes 4 to 6 servings

Hurry Curry Chicken

A dish that looks good, tastes good and is fast. If you don't have any leftover cooked chicken, microwave two large chicken breasts (page 69). While those are cooking, cut and assemble the remaining ingredients. Serve with rice, and you'll have a meal in less than 30 minutes.

2 tbsp	butter	25 mL
1	onion, chopped	1
2	stalks celery, chopped	2
1	small green or red pepper, chopped	1
3 tbsp	all-purpose flour	50 mL
2 tsp	curry powder	10 mL
¼ tsp	salt	1 mL
¼ tsp	freshly ground black pepper	1 mL
1½ cups	chicken stock	375 mL
¼ cup	chutney	50 mL
2 cups	cubed cooked chicken or turkey	500 mL
1	red apple, cored and diced	1

▶ Combine butter, onion, celery and pepper in an 8 cup (2 L) microwavable casserole. Microwave, uncovered, at High (100%) for 2 to 4 minutes, or until vegetables are softened.

▶ Stir in flour, curry powder, salt and pepper and blend well. Microwave, uncovered, at High (100%) for 30 seconds.

▶ Whisk in chicken stock and chutney. Cover and microwave at High (100%) for 3 to 4 minutes, or until sauce boils and thickens. Stir twice during cooking.

▶ Stir in chicken and apple. Cover and microwave at Medium-High (70%) for 5 to 7 minutes, or until heated through. Stir occasionally during cooking. Serve with hot cooked rice.

Makes 4 to 6 servings

Chicken Enchiladas with Green Sauce

This Mexican dish is so delicious, you'll want it as a company special. The canned green tomatoes ("tomatitos verdes") are a Mexican specialty, but fresh tomatoes can be substituted if you can't find the canned ones. For a more authentic taste, fry the tortillas in lard, one at a time, and fill as soon as they are cooked. About 1½ cups (375 mL) leftover cooked turkey can be substituted for the chicken.

1½ lb	chicken pieces, preferably thighs or breasts	750 g
8 oz	cream cheese	250 g
2 cups	cream	500 mL
1	large onion, finely chopped	1
2 tbsp	chopped fresh coriander or parsley	25 mL
6	mild chilies, or 1 green pepper, chopped	6
2	hot peppers or chilies, chopped	2
1	10 oz (284 mL) can green tomatoes, or 2 fresh tomatoes, chopped	1
1	egg, lightly beaten	1
1 tsp	salt	5 mL
½ tsp	freshly ground black pepper	2 mL
12	8 inch (20 cm) flour tortillas	12
⅓ cup	grated Parmesan cheese	75 mL

▶ Arrange chicken pieces in one layer in a shallow microwavable dish. Place meatier portions toward outer edges of dish. Pierce skin in several places and cover with waxed paper. Microwave at High (100%) for 9 to 14 minutes, or until chicken is tender and juices are no longer pink. Reserve pan juices.
▶ When chicken is cool enough to handle, skin and remove meat from bones. Shred meat into small pieces.
▶ While meat is cooling, place cream cheese in a large microwavable bowl and soften at Medium-Low (30%) for 1½ to 2 minutes. Beat until smooth. Gradually beat in cream until smooth. Stir in onions and coriander. Set aside 1 cup (250 mL) sauce for topping.

▶ Add mild chilies, hot peppers, green tomatoes, egg, salt, pepper, shredded chicken and reserved pan juices to remaining sauce mixture and blend well.

▶ On stove top, fry each tortilla in 1 tsp (5 mL) lard for a few seconds each to soften. OR wrap three tortillas in dampened paper towel and place on a microwavable plate or pie plate. Microwave at Medium (50%) for 1½ minutes (30 seconds per tortilla). Repeat with remaining tortillas.

▶ Fill tortillas while still warm and pliable. Reheat if they become too stiff to roll. Place ⅓ cup (75 mL) chicken mixture on each tortilla and roll up. (Although mixture will be thin, it will solidify during cooking.) Place in a single layer in a shallow microwavable dish. Use two 12 × 8 inch (3 L) dishes. Pour reserved sauce over enchiladas and cover with waxed paper.

▶ Microwave each dish at Medium (50%) for 5 to 8 minutes, or until hot. Sprinkle with cheese and serve. If desired, run under preheated broiler to brown the top lightly.

Makes 4 to 6 servings

TIP Heat taco shells at High (100%) for 10 seconds each before filling.

TIP For a quick snack or last-minute appetizer, make nachos. Layer tortilla chips evenly on a microwavable dinner plate. Sprinkle with chopped jalapeño peppers or sliced stuffed green olives. Cover evenly with grated old Cheddar cheese. Cook at Medium (50%) for 1½ to 3 minutes, or until cheese is melted. Serve with taco sauce.

Hoisin Chicken with Sesame Seeds

As an accompaniment to this delicious and addictive dish, heat sake (rice wine) in the microwave in a non-metallic sake carafe for 30 seconds at High (100%) and serve in small sake cups.

4	single chicken breasts, skinned and boned	4
¼ cup	sake, mirin or dry sherry	50 mL
2 tbsp	hoisin sauce	25 mL
2 tbsp	soy sauce	25 mL
1 tsp	granulated sugar	5 mL
1 tsp	sesame oil	5 mL
1 tsp	grated fresh ginger	5 mL
1	clove garlic, minced	1
½ tsp	hot red pepper flakes	2 mL
1 tbsp	sesame seeds	15 mL
2	carrots, thinly sliced on the diagonal	2
2 tsp	cornstarch	10 mL
20	snow peas, trimmed	20

▶ Slice chicken into ½ inch (1 cm) strips.
▶ Combine sake, hoisin sauce, soy sauce, sugar, sesame oil, ginger, garlic and red pepper flakes in a bowl just large enough to hold chicken strips. Toss chicken in marinade to coat. Marinate for 30 minutes at room temperature.
▶ Meanwhile, toast sesame seeds in a small microwavable glass bowl at High (100%) for 1½ to 2 minutes, or until lightly toasted. Stir every 30 seconds, as they burn easily and will continue to brown during standing time. Set aside.
▶ Drain chicken from marinade, reserving marinade. Place chicken strips with carrots in an 8 cup (2 L) microwavable casserole.
▶ Stir cornstarch into marinade until smooth. Pour over chicken and carrots and combine well. Cover and microwave at High (100%) for 4 minutes, stirring at least once partway through. Add snow peas and microwave, covered, at High (100%) for 2 to 4 minutes, or until chicken is tender. Sprinkle sesame seeds on top. Serve with rice.

Makes 4 to 6 servings

Orange Glazed Chicken

A tasty glaze with a bit of spice for those days when a meal has to be on the table in a hurry. If you prefer a crisper skin, run the chicken under the broiler before serving.

2 lb	chicken pieces (6 to 8)	1 kg
1 tbsp	butter	15 mL
2	cloves garlic, minced	2
½ cup	marmalade	125 mL
½ tsp	paprika	2 mL
½ tsp	curry powder	2 mL
¼ tsp	ground cumin	1 mL
¼ tsp	dry mustard	1 mL

▶ Trim excess fat from chicken pieces, and pierce skin in a few places. Arrange on a microwave roasting rack with meatiest parts toward the outer edge of rack or dish.

▶ In a small microwavable bowl, combine butter and garlic. Microwave at High (100%) for 1 minute. Add remaining ingredients and microwave at High (100%) for 1 minute. Stir to blend.

▶ Brush glaze over chicken. Cover with waxed paper and cook at High (100%) for 6 to 8 minutes per pound (500 g), rearranging chicken partway through cooking if necessary. Chicken is done when juices run clear when pierced. Let stand for 5 minutes, then broil, if desired, before serving.

Makes 3 to 4 servings

TIP Whenever you need cooked chicken for a casserole, salad or sandwich, simply place chicken pieces in a single layer in a shallow microwavable dish. Pierce skin in several places with a knife, and cover with vented plastic wrap. Microwave at High (100%) for 6 to 8 minutes per pound (500 g), or until tender and juices are no longer pink when flesh is pierced. Let chicken stand until cool enough to handle, then skin and bone.

Citrus and Spice Grilled Chicken

You can use limes, lemons or oranges in this interesting marinade. Partial cooking in the microwave will prevent the meat from charring during barbecuing. You can also finish the dish under the broiler.

2 lb	chicken pieces (6 to 8)	1 kg
	Grated rind and juice of 1 lemon	
	Grated rind and juice of 1 orange	
1	onion, chopped	1
1	clove garlic, minced	1
1 tsp	freshly ground black pepper	5 mL
1 tsp	dried oregano	5 mL
½ tsp	ground cumin	2 mL
½ tsp	allspice	2 mL

▶ Combine all ingredients in a plastic bag and seal. Refrigerate and marinate for 6 to 24 hours, turning bag often.

▶ Remove chicken pieces from marinade and place in a shallow microwavable dish with meatier portions toward outer edges. Pierce skin in several places. Cover with waxed paper and microwave at High (100%) for 4 minutes per pound (500 g). Reserve marinade.

▶ Transfer chicken to preheated barbecue and grill until golden, turning several times. Baste with marinade during cooking. Juices should run clear when meat is pierced (no trace of pink).

Makes 4 to 6 servings

TIP For easier clean-up, microwave a damp dish cloth at High (100%) for 20 to 30 seconds and use it to wipe up spills and splatters on oven walls.

Moroccan Grilled Chicken

Partial microwaving and final grilling results in moist chicken with a crisp skin. The chunky sauce is a little different, but delicious. Serve with cooked rice.

2 tbsp	butter	25 mL
1	large onion, chopped	1
2	cloves garlic, minced	2
2 tsp	grated fresh ginger	10 mL
2 tsp	curry powder	10 mL
1 tsp	coriander seeds, lightly crushed	5 mL
½ tsp	ground cumin	2 mL
pinch	freshly ground black pepper	pinch
2 lb	chicken pieces (6 to 8)	1 kg
1	lemon, cut into 8 wedges	1
12	stuffed green olives, sliced	12
¼ cup	dark raisins	50 mL

▶ Combine butter, onion, garlic and ginger in a shallow microwavable dish large enough to hold chicken in one layer. Microwave, uncovered, at High (100%) for 2 minutes. Stir in curry, coriander, cumin and pepper. Microwave at High (100%) for 1 minute.
▶ Arrange chicken pieces in dish with thicker meatier portions to outer edges. Pierce skin in several places with a sharp knife. Spoon some of the sauce mixture over chicken and tuck lemon wedges in and around chicken pieces.
▶ Cover with waxed paper and microwave at High (100%) for 4 minutes per pound (500 g).
▶ Remove chicken pieces from sauce and transfer to a preheated barbecue grill or onto a broiler rack. Grill or broil until chicken pieces are cooked through and juices run clear when pieces are pierced.
▶ Meanwhile, discard lemon wedges and add olives and raisins to pan juices. Microwave, uncovered, at High (100%) for 3 to 4 minutes, or until hot. Serve with chicken.

Makes 6 to 8 servings

Shanghai Skewered Chicken

Moist and delicious and just right for two. This recipe can easily be doubled or tripled—use one chicken breast per serving and adjust the cooking time accordingly.
While the chicken is marinating, cook the rice and toss a salad. You'll have a meal in no time!

2	single chicken breasts, skinned and boned	2
2 tbsp	soy sauce	25 mL
1 tbsp	lemon or lime juice	15 mL
1 tbsp	honey	15 mL
1 tsp	grated fresh ginger	5 mL
1	clove garlic, minced	1
½	red pepper, cut into chunks	½
8	mushrooms	8

▶ Cut chicken into ¾ inch (2 cm) pieces. Combine soy sauce, lemon juice, honey, ginger and garlic. Toss chicken with mixture and marinate for 15 minutes.

▶ Thread chicken alternately with red pepper and mushrooms on 4 bamboo skewers. Allow ¼ inch (5 mm) space between chicken and vegetables for even cooking. Arrange skewers in a shallow dish, at least ½ inch (1 cm) apart. Cover loosely with waxed paper and microwave at High (100%) for 3 to 4 minutes, or until chicken is tender and no longer pink. Let stand for 3 minutes. Serve with cooked rice.

Makes 2 servings

TIP Many microwave recipes can be adapted to serve one or two people. Cut down the recipe by halving the ingredients and using a smaller dish to keep the food from spreading out too much and over-cooking. Because cooking time in the microwave depends on the amount of food being cooked, start by microwaving for half the cooking time and then test for doneness. Increase the cooking time as required.

Golden Glazed Cornish Hens

Cornish hens are small and tender—perfect for roasting in the microwave. Use dark soy sauce to give the hens a rich golden color. This glaze can also be used with chicken parts. Brush the chicken with the basting sauce and place in a shallow microwavable dish, placing the thicker, meatier parts toward the outer edges. Microwave at High (100%) for 6 to 8 minutes per pound (500 g). Let stand for 5 to 10 minutes before serving.

2	Cornish hens	2
2	small onions, peeled	2
2	cloves garlic, peeled	2
¼ cup	butter	50 mL
1 tbsp	Dijon mustard	15 mL
1 tbsp	Hot and Sweet Mustard (page 183), or Russian-style mustard	15 mL
1 tbsp	honey	15 mL
1 tbsp	soy sauce	15 mL
1 tsp	lemon juice	5 mL
1	clove garlic, minced	1

▶ Remove giblets from hens. Wash and dry hens. Place an onion and garlic clove in each cavity. Truss each bird with string to form a compact shape. Pierce skin in a few places with a sharp knife.

▶ Melt butter in a small microwavable dish at High (100%) for 30 to 40 seconds. Stir in remaining ingredients until evenly blended.

▶ Brush birds evenly with about three-quarters of basting sauce. Place birds breast side down on microwave roasting rack, at least 1 inch (2.5 cm) apart. Microwave, uncovered, at High (100%) for 6 to 8 minutes per pound (500 g), or until juices run clear when skin is pierced with a knife. Halfway through cooking time, turn birds over and brush with remaining basting mixture.

▶ Cover birds loosely with foil and let stand for 15 minutes to complete cooking. To serve, remove string and cut each hen in half lengthwise.

Makes 4 servings

Turkey Breast with
Apricot Ginger Stuffing

The boned turkey breasts are stuffed with a delicious combination of apricots, ginger, almonds and orange, and are then rolled. This makes a compact shape that will cook perfectly in the microwave— giving you a moist, tender turkey dish. The preparation requires a bit of work and string, but it is worth the extra effort.

2	single turkey breasts—about 1½ lb (750 g) each	2
2 tbsp	butter	25 mL
1	onion, chopped	1
1 tsp	grated fresh ginger	5 mL
2 cups	soft breadcrumbs	500 mL
½ cup	chopped dried apricots	125 mL
¼ cup	sliced almonds	50 mL
2 tbsp	finely chopped parsley	25 mL
	Grated rind and juice of ½ orange	
	Salt and freshly ground black pepper to taste	
GLAZE		
¼ cup	apricot jam	50 mL
2 tbsp	butter	25 mL

▶ Bone turkey breasts, but do not skin. Place between pieces of waxed paper and pound until about ½ inch (1 cm) thick.
▶ Lay breasts side by side, skin side down on a large piece of plastic wrap or waxed paper. (This will make rolling easier later on.) Fit the breasts together to make an oblong or square. Sew the two breasts together in the center of the oblong to make one piece. Sew up any other holes with a few stitches so the stuffing will not fall out. Set aside while making stuffing.
▶ In a 6 cup (1.5 L) microwavable casserole, combine butter, onion and ginger. Microwave at High (100%) for 2 to 3 minutes to soften vegetables. Stir in remaining stuffing ingredients.
▶ Spread stuffing on turkey breasts, leaving a 1 inch (2.5 cm) border on all sides. Starting at the narrow end, use the plastic wrap to help you roll up the turkey jelly-roll fashion, as snugly as possible. Tie with string. (You can refrigerate it at this point.)

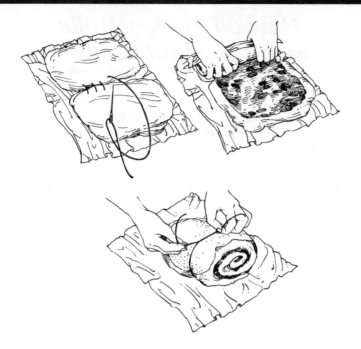

▶ To make the glaze, combine apricot jam and butter in a small microwavable bowl and microwave at High (100%) for 30 to 60 seconds, or until melted and smooth.

▶ Weigh turkey roast, then place on microwave roasting rack. Brush with glaze.

▶ Microwave, uncovered, at Medium-High (70%) for 10 to 11 minutes per pound (500 g). Turn roast over once during cooking and brush with any accumulated drippings. Continue cooking until a thermometer inserted in center reads 175 F (80 C). Cover loosely with foil and let stand for 10 to 15 minutes. During standing time the internal temperature should rise to 185 F (85 C).

▶ To serve, slice and garnish with a sprig of parsley and half an orange slice.

Makes 8 servings

TIP Clarify 1 cup (250 mL) butter in a 2 cup (500 mL) glass measure or bowl by microwaving at Medium-Low (30%) for 2 to 3 minutes, or until just melted. Skim off and discard foam from the top. The milk solids will sink to the bottom and the clear liquid is the clarified butter. Because clarified butter has had the milk solids removed, it doesn't burn easily. It is also useful for people with lactose intolerance. Use it for brushing on grilled foods, in crêpe batters, or for dipping.

Herbed Turkey Rolls with Hazelnut Coating

Turkey scallopini (scallops) are thin slices from the turkey breast. If they are difficult to find, substitute boned and skinned chicken breasts and pound until thin.

4	turkey scallops	4
¼ cup	cream cheese with garlic and herbs (Rondele or Boursin)	50 mL
¼ cup	butter	50 mL
1	egg, lightly beaten	1
⅓ cup	ground hazelnuts	75 mL
¼ cup	dry breadcrumbs	50 mL

▶ Place 1 tbsp (15 mL) cheese in center of each scallop. Fold sides over cheese to make an envelope.

▶ In large microwavable dish or pie plate, melt butter at High (100%) for 40 to 60 seconds.

▶ Whisk egg into melted butter.

▶ Combine ground hazelnuts and breadcrumbs in another shallow microwavable dish or pie plate. Microwave, uncovered, at High (100%) for 2 to 3 minutes, stirring every minute, until lightly toasted. Watch carefully to prevent burning.

▶ Dip each turkey roll in egg mixture, coating well, then into breadcrumb mixture.

▶ Place rolls about 2 inches (5 cm) apart on a microwavable plate or dish, seam side down, and refrigerate for 30 minutes.

▶ To cook, cover with waxed paper and microwave at Medium (50%) for 10 to 12 minutes, or until turkey is no longer pink when cut. Let stand for 5 minutes before serving.

Makes 4 servings

6
Fish and Seafood

The microwave is ideally suited to seafood, because most fish and shellfish are naturally delicate and moist and require minimal cooking.

Fish poaches beautifully in the microwave, and this moist, no-fat cooking method combined with the generally low-fat seafood is perfect for anyone who is watching calories. Seafood can be micro-waved without any liquid, but a small amount often works well as a vehicle for seasonings.

Fish fillets can be microwaved at High (100%) for a minimal cooking time to preserve their moistness. Delicate shellfish such as scallops, clams and mussels are usually steamed or poached at a lower power level to prevent toughening.

The recipes in this chapter range from the very simple Spicy Gingered Fish on a Skewer to rich and elegant dishes such as Turban of Sole with Salmon Mousseline, or Scallops in Pernod Cream Sauce. But they are all fast and easy.

Don't be surprised if you find yourself cooking fish more often, once you discover how fresh seafood can taste when cooked in the microwave.

Seafood Tips

▶ Unless otherwise specified, use fresh or completely defrosted seafood for even cooking.

▶ Use a shallow microwavable dish just large enough to hold the fish fillets or steaks in one layer. Arrange the thicker portions toward the outer edges of the dish, with thinner or smaller pieces in the center.

▶ To steam or poach, cover with vented plastic wrap. A looser covering such as waxed paper is suitable when you want to keep heat in and even out cooking without steaming.

▶ Fish steaks or fillets are cooked at High (100%) for 4 to 5 minutes per pound (500 g), or until the fish is opaque, firm to the touch and flakes easily with a fork. Microwave for the minimum cooking time, then test to avoid overcooking.

▶ Whole fish and shellfish are usually cooked at a lower power such as Medium-High (70%) to prevent toughening.

▶ To thaw seafood, use Defrost or Medium-Low (30%) for a minimum amount of time. As the edges of the food begin to feel warm, remove from the package and run under cold water until completely thawed.

Salmon Steaks on Fresh Greens

Since salmon has such an exquisite flavor, the simplest cooking treatment often gives the most satisfying results. You can serve this with the Haida Sauce or with Hollandaise (page 134), or simply cook the salmon as shown and serve it on its own.

HAIDA SAUCE

¼ cup	light soy sauce	50 mL
1 tbsp	lemon juice	15 mL
1 tsp	granulated sugar	5 mL

SALMON STEAKS

4	salmon steaks, about 8 oz (250 g) each	4
1 tbsp	butter, softened	15 mL
1 tbsp	chopped fresh dill, or 1 tsp (5 mL) dried dill weed	15 mL
	Coarsely ground black pepper	
	Lettuce or other greens	

▶ To make sauce, combine soy sauce, lemon juice and sugar. Let stand for 30 minutes before serving.
▶ Smear both sides of salmon with butter. Arrange salmon steaks in a shallow microwavable dish with the large round ends toward outer edges of dish. Sprinkle with dill and liberal amounts of coarsely ground black pepper.
▶ Cover with vented plastic wrap and microwave at High (100%) for 4 to 5 minutes per pound (500 g), or until color changes to a lighter pink and salmon is opaque. Let stand for 5 minutes.
▶ Place bed of torn lettuce on each plate. Top with a salmon steak and sauce.

Makes 4 servings

Salmon Steaks
with Grapefruit Hollandaise

A delicious change from the traditional lemon Hollandaise. Making the Hollandaise requires attention and vigorous whisking to redistribute the heat to the outer edges of the dish.

4	salmon steaks, about 8 oz (250 g) each	4
¼ cup	grapefruit juice	50 mL
GRAPEFRUIT HOLLANDAISE SAUCE		
½ cup	butter	125 mL
¼ cup	grapefruit juice	50 mL
pinch	dry mustard	pinch
pinch	cayenne	pinch
3	egg yolks, lightly beaten	3
GARNISH		
1	grapefruit, peeled and sectioned	1

▶ Arrange salmon steaks in a shallow microwavable dish with thick, round ends toward the outer edges of dish. Pour ¼ cup (50 mL) grapefruit juice over salmon. Cover dish with vented plastic wrap. Microwave at High (100%) for 4 to 5 minutes per pound (500 g), or until salmon is opaque and firm to touch. Let stand while making sauce.

▶ In a 2 cup (500 mL) glass measure or similar round dish, microwave butter at High (100%) for 40 to 60 seconds, or just until melted. Do not let butter get too hot, or sauce may curdle. Whisk ¼ cup (50 mL) grapefruit juice, dry mustard and cayenne into melted butter. This will cool butter slightly. Whisk egg yolks into butter.

▶ Microwave sauce, uncovered, at Medium-Low (30%) for 1 to 3 minutes, whisking every 30 seconds, until sauce thickens and is creamy. If sauce is overcooked, it will separate. If this happens, whisk 1 to 2 tbsp (15 to 25 mL) cold water into sauce until it returns to a creamy consistency.

▶ To serve, spoon sauce over salmon steaks and garnish with grapefruit sections.

Makes 4 servings

Sole Fillets
with Crab Filling

The delicate flavors of the crab and sole complement each other perfectly in this easy, elegant dish.

1	7 oz (200 g) can crab meat	1
2	green onions, chopped	2
½	small red pepper, chopped	½
2 tbsp	sour cream or plain yogurt	25 mL
2 tsp	lemon juice	10 mL
1 tsp	Dijon mustard	5 mL
¼ cup	finely chopped parsley	50 mL
4	sole fillets, about 1 lb (500 g)	4
¾ cup	dry white wine	175 mL
1 tbsp	butter, softened	15 mL
1 tbsp	all-purpose flour	15 mL
	Salt and freshly ground black pepper to taste	

▶ Combine crab meat, green onions, red pepper, sour cream, lemon juice, mustard and 2 tbsp (25 mL) parsley.

▶ Divide filling between the fish fillets and roll up fillets. Place seam side down in a shallow microwavable dish in a ring formation, leaving the center empty.

▶ Pour the wine over the fish. Cover with lid or vented plastic wrap and microwave at High (100%) for 5 to 6 minutes, or until fish flakes easily with a fork. Do not overcook.

▶ Meanwhile, in small bowl or cup, combine butter and flour with a fork until smooth.

▶ Gently remove fish to a serving plate and cover to keep warm.

▶ Whisk butter-flour mixture into poaching liquid and microwave, uncovered, at High (100%) for 2 to 4 minutes, or until sauce thickens. Stir partway through cooking. Taste and season with salt and pepper. Stir in remaining parsley and pour sauce over the fish rolls.

Makes 4 servings

Turban of Sole
with Salmon Mousseline

This dish is very delicate in flavor and texture, and can also be served as an appetizer. The beautiful pink salmon center contrasts with the white fish. Serve with Hollandaise sauce.

2 lb	sole fillets	1 kg
1 lb	boned and skinned fresh salmon, well chilled	500 g
½ tsp	salt	2 mL
¼ tsp	freshly ground white pepper	1 mL
2 tbsp	chopped fresh dill	25 mL
1 tsp	lemon juice	5 mL
2	eggs whites, well chilled	2
1 cup	whipping cream, well chilled	250 mL
	Hollandaise Sauce (page 134)	

▶ Butter a 9 or 10 inch (23 or 25 cm) microwavable ring mold. Arrange sole fillets in mold, overlapping where necessary, so that the bottom of mold is covered and the ends hang over the top.

▶ The salmon, egg whites and cream should be very cold. Reserve the egg yolks to make the Hollandaise. Cut salmon into small pieces and place in food processor with salt, pepper, dill and lemon juice. Process for about 10 seconds.

▶ Add egg whites and process until very smooth. With machine running, slowly add cream in a thin stream and process until all the cream is absorbed and mousse is very smooth.

▶ Spoon mousse evenly into a fish-lined mold. Fold ends of fish over top.

▶ Cover with vented plastic wrap and microwave at Medium-High (70%) for 16 to 20 minutes, until fish is opaque. If necessary, rotate dish during cooking. Let stand, covered, for 5 minutes.

▶ Drain off accumulated liquid. Turn out onto large platter. Cut into serving pieces. Garnish with a lemon wedge and a sprig of fresh dill. Serve with Hollandaise sauce.

Makes 6 to 8 main-course servings, or 10 to 12 appetizer servings

Sole Véronique

To make this classic French dish, first poach the fish in wine, then use the poaching liquid to make the sauce. Use any mild-flavored fish fillets, such as turbot or cod.

1 lb	sole fillets	500 g
¼ cup	dry white wine	50 mL
2	slices lemon	2
4	sprigs parsley	4
2 tbsp	butter	25 mL
2 tbsp	all-purpose flour	25 mL
pinch	salt	pinch
pinch	freshly ground white pepper	pinch
⅔ cup	light cream	150 mL
1 cup	seedless green grapes	250 mL

▶ Cut fish into serving pieces. Arrange pieces in a single layer in a shallow microwavable dish. Place thicker portions at outer edges.

▶ Pour wine over fish; add lemon slices and parsley. Cover with vented plastic wrap. Microwave at High (100%) for 4 to 5 minutes, or until fish flakes easily with a fork. Pour off poaching liquid and reserve. Discard lemon and parsley. Cover with plastic wrap to keep fish warm while making sauce.

▶ To make sauce, melt butter in a 4 cup (1 L) glass measure at High (100%) for 30 to 60 seconds. Blend in flour, salt and pepper to make a smooth paste. Microwave, uncovered, at High (100%) for 30 seconds.

▶ Gradually whisk in ⅓ cup (75 mL) reserved poaching liquid and all the cream. Microwave, uncovered, at High (100%) for 2 to 3 minutes, or until sauce comes to a boil and thickens. Stir partway through cooking. Stir in grapes.

▶ Uncover fish and drain off any accumulated liquid. Pour sauce over top and microwave, uncovered, at Medium-High (70%) for 1 minute.

Makes 3 to 4 servings

Spicy Gingered Fish on a Skewer

You'll need firm-fleshed fish fillets for this recipe, so the long strips won't fall apart. Ocean perch is a good choice, and it has an attractive red skin. The marinade is also the base for a light but spicy sauce.
Serve this with brown rice and steamed green beans or snow peas.

1 lb	ocean perch fillets, fresh or partially defrosted	500 g
½ cup	dry white wine or vermouth	125 mL
	Grated rind and juice of 1 lime	
1 tsp	grated fresh ginger	5 mL
2	cloves garlic, minced	2
½ tsp	hot red pepper flakes	2 mL
2 tbsp	brown sugar	25 mL
1 tbsp	soy sauce	15 mL
1 tsp	cornstarch	5 mL

▶ If fillets are frozen together, separate under cold running water. They will be easier to cut while still partially frozen and will finish defrosting during marinating. Cut into long strips about ½ inch (1 cm) thick.

▶ Combine wine, grated lime rind and juice, ginger, garlic and hot pepper flakes in a shallow dish large enough to hold the fish strips. Add fish and stir gently to cover with marinade. Marinate at room temperature for 15 to 30 minutes, turning occasionally.

▶ Remove fish from marinade and thread on bamboo skewers. Reserve marinade. Arrange on microwave roasting rack. Cover loosely

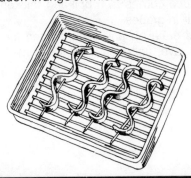

with waxed paper and microwave at High (100%) for 4 to 5 minutes, or until fish is opaque. You may want to rearrange skewers partway through cooking, moving the center ones to the outer edges. Cover and let stand while making sauce.

▶ Pour marinade into a 2 cup (500 mL) glass measure. Stir in brown sugar, soy sauce and cornstarch until smooth. Microwave, uncovered, at High (100%) for 1½ to 2 minutes, or until sauce comes to a boil and thickens slightly. Stir once during cooking. Serve sauce with fish.

Makes 3 to 4 servings

Cajun Cod

Although not "blackened" like some traditional Cajun recipes, this seasoning mixture is wonderfully fiery.

1 lb	cod or halibut fillets	500 g
¼ cup	butter	50 mL
1 tsp	paprika	5 mL
½ tsp	cayenne	2 mL
½ tsp	onion powder	2 mL
½ tsp	garlic powder	2 mL
¼ tsp	salt	1 mL
¼ tsp	freshly ground white pepper	1 mL
¼ tsp	freshly ground black pepper	1 mL
¼ tsp	dried thyme	1 mL
¼ tsp	dried oregano	1 mL

▶ Cut fish into serving pieces. In a glass pie plate or other microwavable flat dish, melt butter at High (100%) for 30 to 60 seconds.
▶ Combine seasonings in a small dish.
▶ Dip both sides of fish pieces into butter, then sprinkle both sides lightly but evenly with seasoning mixture. Arrange fillets on a microwave roasting rack, placing thicker pieces to the outer edges.
▶ Cover loosely with waxed paper and microwave at High (100%) for 4 to 5 minutes, or until fish flakes easily with a fork. Let stand for a few minutes before serving.

Makes 3 to 4 servings

Scallops
in Pernod Cream Sauce

Delicate scallops are best poached at Medium power, to avoid toughening. The poaching liquid becomes the base for the cream sauce. This is a delicious and rich dish to serve for special guests.

1½ lb	sea scallops	750 g
½ cup	dry white wine	125 mL
¼ cup	Pernod	50 mL
2	shallots, chopped	2
2 tbsp	finely chopped parsley	25 mL
pinch	salt	pinch
pinch	freshly ground white pepper	pinch
½ cup	light cream, approx.	125 mL
3 tbsp	butter	50 mL
3 tbsp	all-purpose flour	50 mL
¼ cup	freshly grated Parmesan cheese	50 mL
	Lemon slices	

▶ If you have large scallops, cut them in half or quarters.

▶ Combine wine, Pernod and shallots in an 8 cup (2 L) microwavable casserole. Cover and microwave at High (100%) for 2 to 3 minutes, or until liquid boils.

▶ Gently stir in scallops, 1 tbsp (15 mL) parsley, salt and pepper. Cover and microwave at Medium (50%) for 6 to 8 minutes, stirring gently partway through cooking. Scallops should be just opaque and feel firm. Do not overcook.

▶ Transfer scallops with a slotted spoon to an attractive microwavable serving plate. Cover to keep warm.

▶ Pour poaching liquid into a 2 cup (500 mL) glass measure. Add enough cream to make 1½ cups (375 mL) liquid.

▶ In same 8 cup (2 L) casserole, melt butter at High (100%) for 30 to 60 seconds. Stir in flour and microwave at High (100%) for 30 seconds. Stir in reserved poaching liquid and cream, whisking to make sure no lumps remain on the bottom.

▶ Cover and microwave at High (100%) for 2 to 4 minutes, or until sauce comes to a boil and thickens. Stir partway through cooking.

▶ Drain off any excess liquid that has accumulated around the scal-

lops. Pour sauce evenly over scallops. Sprinkle with Parmesan cheese and remaining parsley.
▶ Microwave at Medium (50%) for 1 to 2 minutes to heat through and melt cheese. Garnish with lemon slices and serve immediately.

Makes 4 to 6 main-course servings, or 8 appetizer servings

Poached Turbot
with Vegetables and Chèvre

This recipe shows off the microwave oven for what it does best—
quick, easy and delicious poached fish with a creamy sauce.

1 lb	firm-fleshed fish such as turbot, cod, sole or ocean perch	500 g
1	tomato, chopped	1
½ cup	chopped green pepper	125 mL
2 tbsp	finely chopped parsley	25 mL
¼ cup	dry white wine or fish stock	50 mL
⅓ cup	light cream	75 mL
½ cup	soft chèvre (goat) cheese, about 3 oz (90 g)	125 mL
	Salt and freshly ground white pepper to taste	

▶ Cut fish into serving pieces. Arrange evenly in a shallow microwavable dish large enough to hold the fish in one layer, placing thicker pieces to the outer edges.
▶ Sprinkle fish evenly with tomato, green pepper and parsley. Pour wine over all and cover with vented plastic wrap. Microwave at High (100%) for 4 to 5 minutes, or until fish flakes easily with a fork. Let stand while making sauce.
▶ In a small microwavable bowl, microwave cream at High (100%) for 30 to 60 seconds, or until hot but not boiling. Stir in chèvre until smooth and melted.
▶ To serve, lift fish and vegetables onto plate with a slotted spoon. Spoon sauce over. Season to taste with salt and pepper.

Makes 3 to 4 servings

Shrimp with Green Peppercorns

Green peppercorns are unripe peppercorn berries. They are usually packed in water or brine and should be drained and rinsed before using. Green peppercorns are milder than dried peppercorns, and can actually be eaten whole.
Serve this colorful dish with lemon wedges—a squeeze of lemon juice will bring out the flavors.

1 lb	raw shrimp	500 g
1	onion, chopped	1
4	stalks celery, thinly sliced on the diagonal	4
¼ cup	chopped red pepper	50 mL
2 tbsp	finely chopped parsley	25 mL
2 tsp	green peppercorns	10 mL
¼ cup	dry vermouth	50 mL
2 tbsp	butter	25 mL
	Salt and freshly ground black pepper to taste	
	Lemon wedges	

▶ Shell and devein shrimp. Place in an 8 cup (2 L) microwavable casserole. Add onion, celery, red pepper and parsley.
▶ Lightly crush peppercorns and add to mixture along with vermouth. Stir well and marinate for 30 minutes at room temperature.
▶ Add butter, cover and microwave at Medium-High (70%) for 6 to 9 minutes, or just until shrimp turn bright pink. Stir twice during cooking. Do not overcook, or shrimp will toughen. Let stand for 5 minutes.
▶ Season with salt and pepper and serve with lemon wedges.

Makes 4 servings

Seafood Kabobs

This dish can also be served as an appetizer—thread on short bamboo skewers to provide each person with a colorful combination. Vary the seafood if you wish.

6	large raw shrimp	6
4 oz	swordfish, halibut or other firm fish	125 g
6	large scallops	6
¼ cup	lemon juce	50 mL
¼ cup	ketchup	50 mL
1 tbsp	soy sauce	15 mL
1	clove garlic, minced	1
1 tbsp	finely chopped parsley	15 mL
1 tsp	grated fresh ginger	5 mL
dash	Tabasco	dash
1	small red or green pepper	1
3	green onions	3

▶ Peel and devein shrimp. Cut fish into six 1 inch (2.5 cm cubes). Place scallops, shrimp and fish in a shallow dish.

▶ Combine remaining ingredients except pepper and green onions. Pour over seafood, cover and refrigerate for 3 to 6 hours.

▶ Cut pepper and onions into 1 inch (2.5 cm) pieces. Alternate on bamboo skewers with seafood. Leave ¼ inch (5 mm) space between pieces.

▶ Place skewers in a shallow dish, cover loosely with waxed paper and microwave at High (100%) for 4 to 6 minutes, or until shrimp turns pink and scallops are opaque. Rotate skewers partway through cooking.

Makes 2 main-course servings, or 4 appetizer servings

Paella

The microwave simplifies this popular Spanish dish. Use fresh clams and mussels in the shell if you can. If you are using frozen shrimp, defrost before adding them to the rice.

6	chicken pieces	6
4	spicy uncooked Italian or Spanish sausages, cut into 1 inch (2.5 cm) pieces, about 1 lb (500 g) total	4
2 cups	short-grain (Arborio) rice	500 mL
1	green pepper, chopped	1
1	onion, chopped	1
1	clove garlic, minced	1
1	tomato, chopped	1
1 tsp	salt	5 mL
½ tsp	freshly ground black pepper	2 mL
½ tsp	saffron or paprika	2 mL
2 cups	hot chicken stock or water	500 mL
6	fresh shrimp, peeled and deveined	6
6	mussels, scrubbed	6
6	clams, scrubbed	6
1 cup	frozen peas	250 mL

▶ In a 16 cup (4 L) microwavable casserole, arrange chicken and sausages. Cover and microwave at Medium-High (70%) for 20 minutes, or until meat is no longer pink. Stir twice during cooking. Remove meat and set aside. Reserve all the cooking liquid.

▶ To the same casserole add rice, vegetables, seasonings and hot stock. Cover and microwave at High (100%) for 15 to 18 minutes, or until most of liquid is absorbed and rice is tender. Stir once partway through cooking.

▶ Stir in shrimp, mussels, clams, peas, chicken and sausages. Cover and microwave at Medium-Low (30%) for 10 to 15 minutes, or until shells are open and peas are cooked. Stir once partway through cooking. Let stand for 5 minutes before serving.

Makes 6 to 8 servings

7
The Lighter Side

The Lighter Side includes an assortment of recipes—egg and cheese dishes, rice and pasta specialties, and salad and luncheon dishes. Some dishes are meant to accompany a main course; some *are* a light main course, delicious for brunch or lunch.

Many egg and cheese dishes work well in the microwave when cooked at a lower power level and watched carefully. Some recipes combine conventional appliances with the microwave, as in the case of the pasta dishes. Other dishes are run under the broiler to produce a browned or crisp top.

Garlic Cheese and Zucchini Quiche

This is a soft, custard-like quiche with a rich, garlic flavor and an attractive green-flecked surface. A tomato salad and crusty bread will round out a brunch or lunch.

1 tbsp	butter, softened	15 mL
¼ cup	dry breadcrumbs	50 mL
3	eggs	3
1 cup	milk	250 mL
4 oz	cream cheese with garlic and herbs (Boursin or Rondele), softened	125 g
1 cup	grated unpeeled zucchini	250 mL

▶ Generously rub sides and bottom of a 9 inch (23 cm) microwavable quiche dish, pie plate or round baking dish with butter. Add the breadcrumbs and shake the dish back and forth to coat the sides and bottom. Pour out the excess crumbs. Refrigerate for 15 minutes to set base.

▶ Meanwhile, in medium bowl, beat eggs lightly. Add milk, cheese and zucchini and beat until evenly blended.

▶ Pour filling into refrigerated base. Microwave, uncovered, at Medium (50%) for 14 to 16 minutes, or until almost set in the center. Rotate dish, if necessary, during cooking.

▶ Let stand directly on counter for 10 minutes before serving.

Makes 4 to 6 servings

Smoked Salmon and Cream Cheese Quiche

This is a creamy rich quiche with a wonderful combination of flavors —smoked salmon, dill and lemon.

1 tbsp	butter, softened	15 mL
¼ cup	dry breadcrumbs	50 mL
2 oz	smoked salmon, finely diced	60 g
2	green onions, chopped	2
8 oz	cream cheese, softened	250 g
3	eggs	3
1 cup	cream	250 mL
2 tbsp	chopped fresh dill, or 1 tsp (5 mL) dried dill weed	25 mL
1 tsp	horseradish	5 mL
½ tsp	grated lemon rind	2 mL
½ tsp	salt	2 mL
¼ tsp	freshly ground black pepper	1 mL

▶ Generously rub the sides and bottom of a 9 inch (23 cm) microwavable quiche dish or pie plate with the butter. Add breadcrumbs and shake dish back and forth to coat sides and bottom. Pour out excess crumbs. Refrigerate for 15 minutes to set.

▶ Sprinkle smoked salmon and green onions over the crumb base.

▶ In a food processor or blender, blend the cream cheese, eggs and cream until smooth. Blend in dill, horseradish, lemon rind, salt and pepper. Pour the filling over salmon and onions.

▶ Microwave, uncovered, at Medium (50%) for 16 to 20 minutes, or until almost set in the center. Rotate dish, if necessary, during cooking. Let stand directly on counter for 10 minutes before serving.

Makes 4 to 6 servings

TIP If you have difficulty cooking the center of a cheesecake or quiche, cut a 2 inch (5 cm) wide donut shape out of foil to fit the circumference of the dish. About halfway through the cooking time, place the foil over the outer 2 inches (5 cm) of the cake. Continue cooking until the center is almost set—it should set completely on standing time.

Tex Mex Tart

The hotness of this quiche-like tart will depend on the "heat" of chilis you use. Buy plain corn tortilla chips (rather than cheese or nacho flavored) and crush them in a food processor or between two pieces of waxed paper with a rolling pin. This makes an attractive dish for a brunch or light dinner.
Serve with a salad and Sangria or a light beer.

CRUST

¼ cup	butter	50 mL
1¼ cups	crushed tortilla chips	300 mL
½ cup	cornmeal	125 mL

FILLING

½ cup	chopped ham	125 mL
½ cup	chopped fresh or canned medium-hot peppers or chilis	125 mL
1	small tomato, diced	1
3	eggs	3
1½ cups	sour cream	375 mL
1 tsp	chili powder	5 mL
½ tsp	ground cumin	2 mL
½ tsp	dried oregano	2 mL

▶ To make crust, in 9 inch (23 cm) microwavable quiche dish, pie plate or round baking dish, melt butter at High (100%) for 40 to 60 seconds. Stir in crushed tortilla chips and cornmeal, blending well. Press against sides and bottom of dish. Microwave at High (100%) for 2 to 3 minutes, or until firm.

▶ Sprinkle ham, peppers and tomato evenly over crust.

▶ In medium bowl, lightly beat eggs. Stir in remaining ingredients until well blended.

▶ Pour egg mixture into crust. Smooth out filling and microwave, uncovered, at Medium (50%) for 16 to 20 minutes, or until almost set in the center. If necessary, rotate dish during cooking. Let stand on counter for 10 minutes—the filling should set during standing time. Serve warm or at room temperature.

Makes 6 servings

Salmon and Asparagus Timbales

These light custards make lovely light appetizers or a light lunch. The microwave eliminates the need for a water bath and reduces the cooking time by half.

2 tbsp	butter	25 mL
3	green onions, chopped	3
4	stalks fresh asparagus, tough ends snapped off, cut into ½ inch (1 cm) pieces	4
1	7¾ oz (220 g) can red salmon, drained	1
5	eggs	5
1 cup	whipping cream	250 mL
1 cup	sour cream	250 mL
1 tbsp	chopped fresh dill, or 1 tsp (5 mL) dried dill weed	15 mL
¼ tsp	salt	1 mL
¼ tsp	freshly ground white pepper	1 mL

▶ In a 4 cup (1 L) microwavable casserole, combine butter and green onions. Microwave, uncovered, at High (100%) for 1 minute.

▶ Stir in asparagus, cover with plastic wrap and microwave at High (100%) for 1 to 2 minutes just to partially cook asparagus.

▶ Break salmon into small pieces and add to asparagus mixture. Divide this mixture evenly between 6 to 8 lightly buttered ramekins or custard cups.

▶ In medium bowl, beat eggs until frothy. Beat in cream, sour cream and seasonings until evenly blended. Pour evenly among ramekins, filling each about three-quarters full. Stir mixture in each ramekin.

▶ Arrange ramekins in a ring formation in microwave. Cover with plastic wrap and microwave at Medium (50%) for 15 to 18 minutes, or until custards are set. If necessary, rearrange cups during cooking to ensure even cooking. Let stand for 5 to 10 minutes before unmolding onto individual serving plates.

Makes 6 to 8 servings

Classic Swiss Fondue

A creamy cheese fondue can be prepared easily in the microwave, without worrying about sticky pots. This makes a nice luncheon or brunch dish, or a starter to a more substantial meal. Reheat the fondue at Medium (50%) to keep warm. Or you may wish to transfer the sauce to a fondue pot and keep it warm over a burner. You can also dip pieces of raw vegetables such as broccoli or cauliflower florets.

1	clove garlic	1
1½ cups	dry white wine	375 mL
8 oz	Emmenthal cheese, grated	250 g
8 oz	Gruyère cheese, grated	250 g
1 tbsp	cornstarch	15 mL
1 tsp	dry mustard	5 mL
2 tbsp	kirsch	25 mL
pinch	freshly ground black pepper	pinch
pinch	ground nutmeg	pinch
	Cubes of French bread, with crust	

▶ Cut garlic in half and rub over sides and bottom of an attractive 8 cup (2 L) microwavable dish. Add wine. Cover and microwave until wine boils, about 3 to 4 minutes at High (100%).

▶ Meanwhile, toss cheeses with cornstarch and mustard until evenly blended. Add cheese mixture to wine a handful at a time, stirring constantly.

▶ Cover and microwave at High (100%) for 1 minute. Stir vigorously and microwave at Medium (50%) for 4 to 6 minutes, or until cheese is smooth. Stir often during cooking time.

▶ Stir in kirsch and seasonings to taste. Serve immediately. Use long-handled forks to dip bread cubes into the fondue.

Makes 4 lunch servings, or 6 appetizer servings

Chili Beer Fondue

A smooth, colorful fondue that makes lunch or brunch for four or appetizers for six to eight. Serve with a variety of vegetables to dip along with tortilla chips and chunks of crusty bread. Make as hot as you like by adding chili peppers.

2 tbsp	butter	25 mL
½	red pepper, finely chopped	½
2 to 4	fresh hot chilis, finely chopped	2 to 4
1	clove garlic, minced	1
2 tbsp	all-purpose flour	25 mL
1	12 oz (341 mL) bottle or can beer	1
3 cups	grated old Cheddar cheese	750 mL
	Fresh vegetables, trimmed (broccoli, cauliflower, mushrooms, zucchini, etc.)	
	Tortilla chips and crusty bread, cut into chunks	

▶ In an 8 cup (2 L) microwavable casserole, combine butter, red pepper, chilis and garlic. Microwave, uncovered, at High (100%) for 2 to 4 minutes, or until vegetables are softened. Stir once during cooking.

▶ Stir in flour and microwave, uncovered, at High (100%) for 30 seconds. Whisk in beer until smooth, cover and microwave at High (100%) for 3 to 5 minutes, or until mixture comes to a boil and thickens. Stir twice during cooking.

▶ Gradually stir cheese into hot sauce to melt. Cover and microwave at Medium (50%) for 1 to 2 minutes, or until cheese melts completely.

▶ Serve immediately with vegetable crudités, tortilla chips and bread chunks.

Makes 4 lunch servings, or 6 to 8 appetizer servings

Vegetable Rice Pilaf

This is similar to a conventional pilaf, but so much easier when made in the microwave! There's no need to worry about sticky rice or scorched pots. This dish has a wonderfully buttery flavor and can be served with just about anything. It is also a good recipe for using up leftover cooked vegetables. Just add them to the casserole after cooking; they will heat through during the standing time.

1 cup	long-grain rice	250 mL
1	onion, sliced	1
¼ cup	butter	50 mL
2 cups	chicken stock	500 mL
2	green onions, sliced	2
1	stalk celery, sliced	1
1	small tomato, chopped	1
2 tbsp	finely chopped parsley	25 mL

▶ Combine rice, onion and butter in an 8 cup (2 L) microwavable casserole. Microwave, uncovered, at High (100%) for 3 to 4 minutes, or until rice is coated with butter. Stir partway through cooking time.
▶ Stir in chicken stock, cover and microwave at High (100%) for 5 minutes. Reduce to Medium (50%) for 10 to 14 minutes, or until most of liquid is absorbed.
▶ Stir in green onions, celery, tomato and parsley and let stand, covered, for 10 to 15 minutes, until remaining liquid is absorbed and vegetables are heated through.

Makes 4 to 6 servings

VARIATION
Curried Rice Pilaf: Add 1 minced clove garlic and 2 tsp (10 mL) curry powder to chicken stock. Replace green onion, celery and tomato with ⅓ cup (75 mL) sliced almonds and increase parsley to ¼ cup (50 mL). Follow directions as above.

Chili Rice

A colorful, zesty side dish to perk up plain grilled meats.

1 cup	long-grain rice	250 mL
1	onion, chopped	1
1	clove garlic, minced	1
2 tbsp	butter	25 mL
1 cup	tomato juice	250 mL
1 cup	water	250 mL
1	4 oz (114 mL) can chopped green chilies	1
1 tsp	chili powder	5 mL
pinch	salt	pinch
pinch	freshly ground black pepper	pinch

▶ Combine rice, onion, garlic and butter in an 8 cup (2 L) microwavable casserole. Cover and microwave at High (100%) for 2 to 3 minutes, or until rice is coated with butter. Stir partway through cooking.

▶ Stir in remaining ingredients. Cover and microwave at High (100%) for 5 minutes. Reduce to Medium (50%) for 10 to 14 minutes, or until most of the liquid is absorbed. Let stand for 10 to 15 minutes before serving.

Makes 4 to 6 servings

TIP To soften flour or corn tortillas for filling and rolling, wrap three tortillas in a dampened paper towel and microwave at Medium (50%) for 1½ minutes (about 30 seconds each).

Risotto

Preparing risotto on the stove is very labor-intensive, as it requires constant stirring. The microwave makes this creamy, richly flavored rice an easy dish to prepare. It is essential to use Italian short-grain rice to achieve the right texture.

1 cup	short-grain rice (preferably Arborio)	250 mL
1 cup	sliced mushrooms	250 mL
1	onion, chopped	1
¼ cup	butter	50 mL
2 cups	chicken stock	500 mL
½ cup	grated Parmesan cheese	125 mL
	Freshly ground black pepper to taste	

▶ Combine rice, mushrooms, onion and butter in an 8 cup (2 L) microwavable casserole. Microwave, uncovered, at High (100%) for 4 to 5 minutes, or until onions are soft. Stir once partway through cooking.

▶ Stir in chicken stock, cover and microwave at High (100%) for 5 minutes, then at Medium (50%) for 8 to 12 minutes, or until most of liquid is absorbed.

▶ Stir, cover and let stand for 5 to 10 minutes, or until all the liquid is absorbed. Stir in Parmesan cheese and pepper and serve immediately.

Makes 4 to 6 servings

Risotto
with Prosciutto and Peas

Also known as Risi e Bisi, *or braised rice and peas, this creamy risotto becomes a light meal in itself.*

1 cup	short-grain rice (preferably Arborio)	250 mL
1	onion, chopped	1
2 tbsp	butter	25 mL
2 cups	chicken stock	500 mL
1 cup	frozen peas, partially thawed	250 mL
2	thin slices prosciutto or smoked ham, diced	2
½ cup	grated Parmesan cheese	125 mL
	Freshly ground black pepper to taste	

▶ Combine rice, onion and butter in an 8 cup (2 L) microwavable casserole. Microwave, uncovered, at High (100%) for 3 to 4 minutes, until rice is coated with butter. Stir partway through cooking time.

▶ Stir in chicken stock, cover and microwave at High (100%) for 5 minutes, then at Medium (50%) for 10 to 14 minutes, or until most of the liquid has been absorbed.

▶ Stir in peas and prosciutto and let stand for 10 minutes to heat peas. Sprinkle with Parmesan cheese and pepper and serve immediately.

Makes 4 to 6 servings

TIP Most foods taste better served warm or at room temperature, rather than cold from the refrigerator. Microwave cheese, grapefruit halves, muffins, slices of pie, sake or brandy. Use Medium (50%) or Medium-Low (30%) to warm briefly.

Fettuccine Primavera

Cook the pasta on the stove while the remaining ingredients and sauce are cooking in the microwave. You can use any combination of vegetables in this recipe—vary the ingredients depending on what you have on hand.

8 oz	dried fettuccine	250 g
¼ cup	butter	50 mL
1	carrot, cut into julienne strips	1
1	zucchini, cut into julienne strips	1
½ cup	·cauliflower florets	125 mL
½ cup	broccoli florets	125 mL
12	snow peas	12
1	red or green pepper, slivered	1
1 cup	whipping cream	250 mL
1	clove garlic, smashed	1
½ cup	grated Parmesan cheese	125 mL
1 tbsp	finely chopped parsley	15 mL
	Salt and freshly ground black pepper to taste	

▶ On the stove, bring a large saucepan of salted water to a boil. Add fettuccine, return to a boil and boil for 8 to 10 minutes, or until pasta is just tender.

▶ Meanwhile, place half the butter in an 8 cup (2 L) microwavable casserole and microwave at High (100%) for 30 to 40 seconds, or until melted. Add the vegetables and toss. Cover with lid or vented plastic wrap and microwave at High (100%) for 5 to 7 minutes, or until vegetables are tender-crisp. Set aside.

▶ Measure cream in a 2 cup (500 mL) glass measure and add garlic. Microwave at High (100%) for 2 minutes, or until cream starts to boil. Remove garlic.

▶ Drain pasta and toss with remaining butter, cream, vegetables, cheese and parsley. Season to taste with salt and pepper. If mixture is cool, microwave at High (100%) for 1 to 2 minutes, or until hot.

Makes 4 servings

Veal-stuffed Pasta with Cream Sauce

Dried pasta tubes are easy to fill when uncooked. Use regular dried cannelloni or manicotti tubes in this recipe—they will rehydrate during cooking. If you are preparing this dish ahead of time, reheat at High (100%) for 5 to 8 minutes.

1 lb	ground veal	500 g
1	onion, chopped	1
4	sprigs parsley	4
1 cup	fresh spinach leaves, well-packed	250 mL
½ tsp	salt	2 mL
½ tsp	dried rosemary	2 mL
½ tsp	ground nutmeg	2 mL
¼ tsp	freshly ground black pepper	1 mL
16	uncooked, dried cannelloni tubes	16
1½ cups	water	375 mL
½ cup	cream	125 mL
¼ cup	dry white wine	50 mL
2 tbsp	tomato paste	25 mL

▶ Combine veal and onion in a 4 cup (1 L) microwavable casserole. Microwave, uncovered, at High (100%) for 3 to 5 minutes, or until the pink color just disappears. Stir frequently during cooking to keep the meat crumbly and cook evenly.

▶ Chop parsley and spinach in food processor or blender. Add veal and onion mixture, salt, rosemary, nutmeg and pepper, and blend well. Pack mixture into the pasta tubes and arrange in an even layer in a 12 × 8 inch (3 L) microwavable dish.

▶ In a medium bowl, combine water, cream, wine and tomato paste. Pour over the pasta. The pasta should be covered with liquid—add more water if necessary. The pasta will absorb most of the liquid, with a small amount remaining to form a creamy sauce.

▶ Cover tightly with plastic wrap and microwave at High (100%) for 16 to 20 minutes, or until pasta is tender. Let stand for 5 minutes. Serve with sauce spooned over top and garnish with chopped parsley.

Makes 4 servings

Spinach Cannelloni with Cheese Filling and Mushroom Sauce

Delicious and rich, and the color contrast of the green pasta with the white filling and mushroom sauce is very attractive. Assemble this dish ahead of time and refrigerate, covered. When cooking, add 2 to 4 minutes to the final cooking time at Medium-High (70%).

8 or 9	fresh or dried spinach lasagna noodles	8 or 9
FILLING		
1½ cups	ricotta cheese	375 mL
¾ cup	grated brick or farmer's cheese	175 mL
½ cup	grated Parmesan cheese	125 mL
1	small onion, finely chopped	1
1	egg, lightly beaten	1
pinch	salt	pinch
pinch	freshly ground white pepper	pinch
SAUCE		
¼ cup	butter	50 mL
1½ cups	sliced mushrooms	375 mL
¼ cup	all-purpose flour	50 mL
pinch	salt	pinch
pinch	freshly ground white pepper	pinch
1 cup	chicken stock	250 mL
½ cup	cream	125 mL
2 tbsp	dry vermouth	25 mL
½ cup	grated Parmesan cheese	125 mL

▶ Cut pasta into pieces approximately 2 × 3½ inches (5 × 9 cm). Bring salted water to a boil in a large saucepan on top of the stove. Drop six pasta pieces into boiling water, one at a time. Cook only until they rise to the surface, about 30 seconds. With a slotted spoon, transfer to a large bowl of cold water. Repeat with all pasta, then drain and lay out on tea towels. (If using dried pasta, cook just until tender before cutting.)

▶ Combine all filling ingredients in large bowl until smooth. Place about 1 tbsp (15 mL) on the narrow end of pasta piece, roll up and place seam side down in a 12 × 8 inch (3 L) microwavable dish. (You should have three rows of 8 or 9 each, depending on how much filling you put in each.) Cover with plastic wrap and set aside while making sauce.

▶ In a 4 cup (1 L) glass measure, combine butter and mushrooms. Microwave, uncovered, at High (100%) for 1½ to 2 minutes, or until mushrooms are softened. Stir partway through cooking.

▶ Stir in flour, salt and pepper and microwave, uncovered, at High (100%) for 30 seconds. Gradually whisk in chicken stock, then blend in cream and vermouth until smooth. Microwave, uncovered, at High (100%) for 3 to 5 minutes, or until mixture comes to a boil and thickens. Stir at least once partway through cooking.

▶ Pour sauce evenly over cannelloni. Cover with vented plastic wrap and microwave at Medium-High (70%) for 12 to 14 minutes, or until hot throughout. Sprinkle with Parmesan cheese, re-cover and let stand for 5 minutes.

Makes 6 main-course servings, or 8 appetizer servings

TIP When recipes refer to vented plastic wrap, cover dish with micro-wavable plastic wrap, turning back a small edge to allow excess steam to escape. When removing wrap or lid after cooking, open the side farthest away from you to avoid steam burns.

Pasta with Peppers and Sausage

A hearty mixture of sausage, green pepper and sun-dried tomatoes. Serve with a dry red wine such as a Valpolicella.

12 oz	dried rigatoni or rotini pasta	375 g
12 oz	Italian sausage, hot or sweet	375 g
1	onion, diced	1
2	cloves garlic, minced	2
1	green pepper, cut into ½ inch (1 cm) pieces	1
¼ cup	chopped sun-dried tomatoes	50 mL
½ cup	dry red wine	125 mL
1 tbsp	tomato paste	15 mL
½ tsp	hot red pepper flakes	2 mL
½ cup	grated Parmesan cheese	125 mL

▶ On the stove, bring a large pot of salted water to a boil. Add pasta, return to a boil and cook for 8 to 10 minutes, or until pasta is tender but firm.

▶ Meanwhile, slice sausage into ½ inch (1 cm) pieces. Combine with onion and garlic in an 8 cup (2 L) microwavable casserole. Microwave, uncovered, at High (100%) for 4 minutes, stirring partway through cooking.

▶ Stir in green pepper, sun-dried tomatoes, red wine, tomato paste and red pepper flakes. Cover and microwave at Medium (50%) for 6 to 8 minutes, until sausage is cooked and vegetables are tender. Stir once during cooking. Let stand, covered, while pasta is finishing.

▶ Drain pasta and place in a large pasta bowl or platter. Add sausage mixture and toss well. Top with Parmesan cheese.

Makes 4 servings

Curried Rice Salad

This is a favorite summer buffet salad. Its mild curry flavor goes well with most meats. If you wish, you can substitute ½ cup (125 mL) chopped smoked ham for the bacon.

8	slices bacon	8
1 cup	long-grain rice	250 mL
2 cups	chicken stock or water	500 mL
1½ tsp	curry powder	7 mL
¼ tsp	salt	1 mL
¼ tsp	freshly ground black pepper	1 mL
1 tsp	lemon juice	5 mL
⅓ cup	mayonnaise or Creamy Salad Dressing (page 136)	75 mL
4	green onions, sliced	4
2 tbsp	finely chopped parsley	25 mL

▶ Arrange the bacon slices between double layers of paper towels and microwave at High (100%) for 5 to 8 minutes, or until crisp. Set aside.

▶ Combine rice, chicken stock, curry powder, salt and pepper in an 8 cup (2 L) microwavable casserole. Cover and microwave at High (100%) for 5 minutes.

▶ Reduce to Medium (50%) and microwave for 10 to 14 minutes, or until most of liquid is absorbed. Let stand for 15 to 20 minutes, or until all liquid is absorbed. Refrigerate to cool.

▶ When rice is cold, fluff with fork. Lightly blend in lemon juice and mayonnaise. Crumble bacon and gently stir in with green onions and parsley. Cover and chill for a few hours before serving.

Makes 6 to 8 servings on a buffet table with other salads

TIP Freeze leftover tomato paste on a waxed paper-lined cookie sheet in 1 tbsp (15 mL) amounts. When frozen, transfer to a freezer bag or container. Defrost in the microwave when small amounts are needed in a recipe.

Chicken Cantaloupe Salad

This salad makes a lovely summer lunch dish. Prepare it early in the day and chill before serving, so that the flavors have time to blend. Use spinach, endive, escarole or spring leaf lettuce for a colorful serving bed.

1 lb	chicken breasts or thighs	500 g
¼ tsp	freshly ground black pepper	1 mL
½ tsp	ground nutmeg	2 mL
2 tsp	sesame seeds	10 mL
¼ cup	mayonnaise or Creamy Salad Dressing (page 136)	50 mL
2 tsp	grated fresh ginger	10 mL
½ tsp	salt	2 mL
½ tsp	dry mustard	2 mL
	Lettuce, spinach, endive or escarole leaves	
2 cups	diced ripe cantaloupe	500 mL

▶ Remove skin from chicken, then sprinkle with pepper and ¼ tsp (1 mL) nutmeg. Arrange in one layer in a shallow microwavable dish with meatier portions toward the outer edges of dish. Cover with waxed paper and microwave at High (100%) for 6 to 8 minutes per pound (500 g), or until chicken is tender and juices run clear when meat is pierced. Cool.

▶ In small glass measure or microwavable dish, microwave sesame seeds, uncovered, at High (100%) for 1 to 3 minutes, or until toasted. Shake or stir during cooking and watch carefully to prevent burning. (The seeds will continue to brown during standing time.)

▶ When chicken is cool enough to handle, remove meat from bone, dice coarsely and place in large bowl.

▶ In small bowl or cup, blend together mayonnaise, ginger, salt, remaining nutmeg and mustard. Combine with chicken. Cover and chill until serving time.

▶ To serve, arrange chicken on a platter lined with lettuce leaves. Place diced cantaloupe in a ring around chicken. Sprinkle with toasted sesame seeds.

Makes 4 servings

Omelet Salad

A colorful light salad just right for lunch. The asparagus and beans will cook in the water that clings to them after washing. To get the right texture, make only two-egg omelets at a time—make the recipe twice for four servings.
To make a quick vinaigrette dressing, combine 4 tsp (20 mL) olive oil, 1½ tsp (7 mL) wine vinegar and a pinch each of salt and pepper.

2 tsp	butter	10 mL
2	eggs, beaten	2
6	asparagus spears, washed and cut into ½ inch (1 cm) pieces	6
12	green beans, washed and cut into ½ inch (1 cm) pieces	12
3	green onions, sliced	3
¼ cup	slivered red pepper	50 mL
2 tbsp	vinaigrette dressing	25 mL
	Lettuce leaves, optional	

▶ In a 9 inch (23 cm) glass pie plate, melt butter at High (100%) for 20 to 40 seconds. Spread over bottom of the plate.
▶ Add eggs, cover with plastic wrap and microwave at Medium (50%) for 2 to 3 minutes. Stir as soon as egg appears to thicken, then cook only until firm. Let stand until cool.
▶ Combine asparagus and beans in a small microwavable dish, cover with plastic wrap and microwave at High (100%) for 2 to 4 minutes, or until tender-crisp. Allow to cool.
▶ Roll omelet into a log and slice into narrow strips. Toss with asparagus, beans, green onions, red pepper and dressing. Serve on lettuce leaves, if desired.

Makes 2 servings

TIP To toast sesame seeds, place ¼ cup (50 mL) in a small glass dish and microwave, uncovered, at High (100%) for 2 to 4 minutes, until lightly toasted. Stir or shake the dish twice during cooking. The seeds will continue to brown during standing time.

Warm Cantonese Chicken Salad

The warm chicken strips top shredded greens for a nice combination of temperature and texture.

1 lb	boneless, skinned chicken breasts	500 g
1 tsp	grated fresh ginger	5 mL
1	clove garlic, minced	1
1 tbsp	sesame oil	15 mL
1 tbsp	soy sauce	15 mL
1 tsp	hoisin sauce	5 mL
2 cups	shredded endive, Romaine or other greens	500 mL
4	green onions, sliced	4
1 tbsp	rice vinegar	15 mL

▶ Cut chicken into long slivers. Toss with ginger, garlic, sesame oil, soy sauce and hoisin sauce in a 4 cup (1 L) microwavable casserole.
▶ Cover loosely with waxed paper and microwave at High (100%) for 4 minutes. Stir once during cooking.
▶ Meanwhile line a serving dish or individual dinner plates with shredded greens.
▶ Add green onions and rice vinegar to chicken mixture and micro-wave, covered, at High (100%) for 1 to 3 minutes, or until chicken is tender and no longer pink.
▶ Spoon chicken over greens and serve warm.

Makes 2 lunch servings, or 4 appetizer servings

TIP To heat 1 cup (250 mL) cold milk or formula in a glass baby bottle, remove cap and nipple from bottle. Microwave at Medium (50%) for 30 to 60 seconds. Replace nipple, shake gently and let stand for 1 minute before testing temperature on wrist.

Picadillo-stuffed Zucchini

This traditional Mexican filling for green peppers or tacos makes a delicious filling for zucchini. Serve with rice to complete the meal.

8 oz	ground beef	250 g
1	onion, chopped	1
2	9 inch (23 cm) zucchini	2
½ tsp	cinnamon	2 mL
½ tsp	ground nutmeg	2 mL
¼ tsp	ground cloves	1 mL
¼ tsp	salt	1 mL
¼ tsp	freshly ground black pepper	1 mL
1 tbsp	finely chopped parsley or coriander	15 mL
1	orange	1
1	tomato, chopped	1
1	sweet banana pepper, chopped	1
1 to 2 tbsp	chopped jalapeño or chili peppers	15 to 25 mL
4	green olives, chopped	4
¼ cup	raisins	50 mL
2 tbsp	slivered almonds	25 mL

▶ In a 6 cup (1.5 L) microwavable bowl or casserole, crumble ground beef with onion. Microwave, uncovered, at Medium-High (70%) for 3 to 5 minutes, or until meat just loses its pink color. Stir once or twice to keep meat from clumping.

▶ Meanwhile, cut zucchini in half lengthwise. Scoop out the centers using a spoon (save for ratatouille, page 128). Arrange zucchini halves in a shallow microwavable dish.

▶ Season meat with cinnamon, nutmeg, cloves, salt, pepper and parsley and stir to combine.

▶ Grate rind from orange and add to meat mixture. Peel remaining pith from orange. Chop orange and add to meat along with remaining ingredients. Spoon into zucchini halves.

▶ Cover with vented plastic wrap and microwave at High (100%) for 8 to 10 minutes, or until zucchini are tender. Rearrange zucchini if necessary during cooking.

Makes 4 servings

8
Vegetables

Vegetables taste so much better when freshly picked. So we developed many of these recipes during the summer months, when we were inspired by the luscious and abundant produce in our gardens and markets.

The microwave oven cooks vegetables to perfection. Green and leafy vegetables can be steamed with a minimum amount of water; potatoes, rutabaga, squash and eggplant can be cooked whole. Simply pierce the skins, and these vegetables will cook in their own moisture. Not only does the microwave cook vegetables quickly, but they will have a better flavor and color, and retain more of their nutrients than with conventional cooking methods. Cabbage and Brussels sprouts can be cooked beautifully without getting soggy or smelly. Beets and sweet potatoes can be cooked more quickly than with stove-top or oven cooking. The microwave also intensifies the natural good taste of vegetables, so that often a bit of butter and a sprinkle of salt and pepper is sufficient seasoning.

Cooking vegetables in the microwave is so easy that you'll be encouraged to experiment. Try something different, like Gingered Parsnips or Kohlrabi with Dill Sauce. Or use up all your vegetable odds and ends in a Vegetable Stir-Fry or Glazed Mélange.

Vegetable Tips

▶ Cut vegetables into uniform pieces for even cooking.

▶ Wash vegetables well—most can be cooked in the moisture that adheres to them after washing. A few of the more fibrous vegetables—green or wax beans, carrots or turnips—are more successfully cooked with a little added water. Use 2 to 4 tbsp (25 to 50 mL) per pound (500 g). This also applies to vegetables a little past their peak. A sprinkle of water will help to soften them.

▶ Avoid sprinkling salt directly on vegetables before cooking. Salt attracts microwaves and may produce an undesirable texture.

▶ By arranging vegetables carefully, additional handling and rearranging can be eliminated. For example, place broccoli with stalks toward outer edges of a round dish and florets in the center. Arrange asparagus in a shallow rectangular dish with stalks at outer edges and tips overlapping in the center.

▶ When cooking whole vegetables with skins—potatoes, beets, turnips, squash, rutabaga, etc.—pierce in several places with a sharp knife to allow steam to escape. Place on a double thickness of paper towels to absorb moisture.

▶ Peeled or cut-up vegetables should be cooked covered, so they will steam as quickly and evenly as possible. Use a tight-fitting casserole lid or plastic wrap. Stir or shake cut vegetables partway through cooking and check after the minimum cooking time. Cook just until tender-crisp and allow adequate standing time—keep covered during standing time.

▶ Most vegetables can be cooked at High (100%). Less tender vegetables or those a little past their prime may be better when cooked at Medium-High (70%) or Medium (50%).

▶ To simplify cooking and peeling rutabagas, microwave them whole to soften and eliminate the difficult and long boiling time. Pierce rutabaga in several places with a small knife. Place on a double thickness of paper towels to catch drippings from wax coating. Microwave a small rutabaga at High (100%) for 10 to 14 minutes, or until tender when pierced with a knife. Turn over partway through cooking. Wrap rutabaga completely with foil and let stand 15 to 20 minutes. Peel, then mash and season to taste.

▶ Cook squash or pumpkin quickly and easily in the microwave. Pierce the skin well in several places with a sharp knife. Place on paper towels or a microwavable plate for easier handling. The cooking time will vary with the type and size of squash, but as a guide, cook at High (100%) for 5 to 8 minutes per pound (500 g), or until a knife pierces easily, and the skin is soft, looks wet, and has darkened in color. Turn the squash over partway through the cooking time. Wrap in foil and let stand for 10 to 15 minutes, or until cool enough to handle. Then cut in half, remove the seeds and scoop out the flesh.

Each pound (500 g) of squash or pumpkin will yield about 1 cup (250 mL) puree. To serve, flavor with any of the following: butter, brown sugar, honey, maple syrup, ginger, cinnamon, nutmeg, fennel seeds, orange juice or grated orange rind, rum, brandy or chopped nuts. The puree can also be used in pie fillings.

▶ To toast pumpkin seeds in the microwave, wash the seeds and pat dry. Place 1 cup (250 mL) seeds in a single layer in a shallow microwavable dish or pie plate. Sprinkle lightly with salt. Microwave, uncovered, at High (100%) for 6 to 8 minutes, or until lightly toasted. Stir every 2 minutes and watch carefully to prevent burning.

Green Beans and Bacon

Fresh green beans are always a treat, but when combined with bacon, they become special.

4	slices bacon, diced	4
1 lb	green beans	500 g
1	onion, chopped	1

▶ Spread diced bacon evenly in a 6 cup (1.5 L) microwavable casserole. Cover with paper towel to prevent splattering. Microwave at Medium (50%) for 3 to 5 minutes, or until crisp. Stir partway through cooking so pieces remain separate. Remove bacon from casserole with slotted spoon. Drain on more paper towels and reserve.
▶ Wash and trim beans. Cut diagonally into 2 inch (5 cm) pieces. Combine with onion and bacon fat in casserole.
▶ Cover and microwave at Medium-High (70%) for 7 to 9 minutes, or until beans are tender. Stir or shake dish partway through cooking time. Top with bacon pieces and let stand for a few minutes before serving.

Makes 4 to 6 servings

Curried Cauliflower

Add some zip to cauliflower. You can use more or hotter curry if you wish. The yogurt makes an easy sauce and adds a nice cooling touch. The aroma will bring everyone to the table.

1 tbsp	olive oil	15 mL
1 to 2 tsp	curry powder	5 to 10 mL
1 lb	cauliflower, cut into florets	500 g
1	large onion, chopped	1
1	small clove garlic, minced	1
½ cup	plain yogurt	125 mL
1 tbsp	finely chopped parsley	15 mL

▶ In a heavy 8 cup (2 L) microwavable casserole, combine oil and curry powder. Tip casserole to keep oil in one corner by placing a small dish or saucer under the opposite corner of casserole in the microwave.

▶ Microwave, uncovered, at High (100%) for 2 minutes to cook the curry. Remove wedge from under casserole.

▶ Toss cauliflower, onion and garlic in curry mixture. Cover and microwave at High (100%) for 8 to 10 minutes, or until cauliflower is tender. Top with yogurt and let stand for 3 to 5 minutes before serving. Sprinkle on parsley.

Makes 4 to 6 servings

Braised Red Cabbage

Cabbage retains its color and has a crunchier texture when cooked in the microwave oven. This recipe is from Kirsten Hamm. It is delicious hot or cold, served with roast pork or turkey.

2 tbsp	butter	25 mL
1	onion, diced	1
½	red cabbage, shredded, about 8 cups (2 L)	½
2 tbsp	red wine vinegar	25 mL
½ tsp	salt	5 mL
⅓ cup	red currant jelly	75 mL

▶ Combine butter and onion in an 8 cup (2 L) microwavable casserole. Microwave at High (100%) for 2 to 3 minutes, or until onion is softened.

▶ Stir in cabbage, vinegar and salt. Cover and microwave at High (100%) for 5 minutes, stirring partway through cooking.

▶ Stir in red currant jelly and microwave, covered, at High (100%) for 5 to 7 minutes, or until cabbage is tender-crisp. Stir partway through cooking time. Let stand for 5 minutes before serving.

Makes 6 servings

Broccoli with Chèvre Sauce

Try broccoli with chèvre (goat cheese) as a change from Cheddar cheese sauce. Remember to undercook the broccoli slightly in the microwave to retain the bright-green color and crispness, as it will cook further under the broiler. For even cooking, arrange the broccoli with stalks toward the outer edges of a round dish, and the florets in the center.

1 lb	broccoli	500 g
½ cup	crumbled chèvre or ricotta cheese	125 mL
⅓ cup	grated Parmesan cheese	75 mL
1	egg, lightly beaten	1
½ cup	whipping cream	125 mL
¼ tsp	freshly ground black pepper	1 mL
2 tbsp	sliced almonds	25 mL

▶ Wash broccoli and cut into florets. Arrange evenly in a round shallow broiler-safe microwavable dish or casserole (the water clinging to the broccoli is sufficient for cooking). Cover with lid or plastic wrap.

▶ Microwave at High (100%) for 3 to 5 minutes, or until just partially cooked. The broccoli should be bright-green but still quite firm.

▶ Meanwhile, place oven rack 6 inches (15 cm) below the broiler element and preheat broiler. Combine remaining ingredients except almonds.

▶ Spoon cheese mixture evenly over broccoli. Sprinkle with almonds.

▶ Cook, uncovered, under broiler for 3 to 4 minutes, or until almonds are golden-brown. Serve immediately.

Makes 4 servings

TIP To make squash easier to cut and peel, microwave at High (100%) for 2 to 3 minutes, or until soft.

Braised Fennel

The addition of Pernod brings out the anise flavor of the fennel. Herbes de Provence is a blend of dried herbs—thyme, marjoram, sage, fennel seed, rosemary and bay leaf. Use a combination of any of these herbs as a substitute.

3	bulbs fennel, about 1 lb (500 g) each	3
2 tbsp	olive oil	25 mL
1	onion, chopped	1
2	cloves garlic, minced	2
2 tbsp	lemon juice	25 mL
1 tsp	Herbes de Provence	5 mL
½ tsp	salt	2 mL
pinch	freshly ground black pepper	pinch
½ tsp	granulated sugar	2 mL
1	tomato, chopped	1
1 tbsp	Pernod	15 mL
¼ cup	grated Parmesan cheese	50 mL

▶ Trim leafy upper stalks from fennel and remove outer leaves. Cut bulbs in half lengthwise and slice.

▶ In an 8 cup (2 L) microwavable casserole, combine oil, onion, garlic and fennel. Microwave, uncovered, at High (100%) for 5 minutes to partially soften vegetables. Stir once during cooking.

▶ Stir in lemon juice, seasonings and tomato. Cover and microwave at High (100%) for 5 to 8 minutes, or until fennel is tender. Stir at least once during cooking.

▶ Stir in Pernod, sprinkle with cheese and let stand, covered, for 5 minutes.

Makes 4 to 6 servings

Brussels Sprouts with Ginger and Cashews

Good with roast turkey or chicken, these crunchy Brussels sprouts could become part of your Thanksgiving tradition.

½ cup	chopped cashews	125 mL
1 lb	Brussels sprouts	500 g
¼ tsp	ground ginger	1 mL

▶ To toast cashews, spread out on a glass pie plate and microwave, uncovered, at High (100%) for 2 to 3 minutes, until fragrant and lightly toasted. Shake dish occasionally during cooking, and watch carefully to avoid burning.

▶ Trim outer leaves from sprouts. Cut an "x" in stem end of each sprout. Soak in salted water for 10 minutes. Drain.

▶ In a 6 cup (1.5 L) casserole, combine Brussels sprouts with ¼ cup (50 mL) water. Cover with casserole lid or plastic wrap. Microwave at High (100%) for 8 to 10 minutes, or until tender-crisp. Stir at least once during cooking. Drain well and toss with cashews and ginger. Let stand 5 minutes.

Serves 6

Julienned Carrots with Horseradish

These carrots are sweet and delicious, with an unusual nippy flavor. They are especially good served with roast pork or beef. If you are using old carrots, add an additional tablespoon (15 mL) water.

4	carrots, cut into julienne strips	4
1	onion, thinly sliced	1
1 tbsp	granulated sugar	15 mL
1 tbsp	horseradish	15 mL
1 tbsp	water	15 mL
1 tbsp	butter	15 mL

▶ Combine carrots and onion in a 6 cup (1.5 L) microwavable casserole. Stir sugar, horseradish and water into vegetables. Cut butter into small pieces and dot vegetables with the pieces.

▶ Cover with lid or vented plastic wrap and microwave at High (100%) for 7 to 10 minutes, or until carrots are tender. Stir or shake dish partway through cooking. Let stand for 5 minutes before serving.

Makes 4 servings

Marmalade Glazed Carrots

A simple recipe that's good with roast pork or chicken. Specialty marmalades such as orange marmalade with malt whisky will make this even more special and elegant.

2 tbsp	orange marmalade	25 mL
2 tbsp	butter	25 mL
6	carrots, cut into julienne strips	6
	Freshly ground black pepper	

▶ In a 6 cup (1.5 L) microwavable casserole, combine marmalade and butter. Microwave, uncovered, at High (100%) for 30 to 60 seconds, or until butter is melted.

▶ Add carrots and toss until coated with mixture. Cover and microwave at High (100%) for 8 to 10 minutes, or until carrots are tender. Stir or shake dish partway through cooking. Season generously with pepper. Let stand for 5 minutes before serving.

Makes 4 to 6 servings

Kohlrabi with Dill Sauce

Kohlrabi grows easily in summer, with pale-green balls that sit above the soil. Inside they are white, and they have a gentle flavor. They can replace potatoes when you want something different.

4	kohlrabi	4
2 tbsp	water	25 mL
2 tbsp	butter	25 mL
2 tbsp	all-purpose flour	25 mL
¾ cup	milk	175 mL
¼ tsp	salt	1 mL
¼ tsp	freshly ground white pepper	1 mL
2 tsp	chopped fresh dill, or 1 tsp (5 mL) dried dill weed	10 mL

▶ Peel kohlrabi to remove skin and coarse surface flesh. Dice or cut into julienne strips. Place in a 6 cup (1.5 L) microwavable casserole and add water.

▶ Cover and microwave at High (100%) for 8 to 10 minutes, or until almost tender. The kohlrabi will continue to cook while sauce is being prepared.

▶ In a 2 cup (500 mL) glass measure, melt butter at High (100%) for 20 to 30 seconds. Stir in flour and microwave at High (100%) for 30 seconds.

▶ Whisk in milk. Microwave, uncovered, at High (100%) for 2 to 3 minutes, or until sauce comes to a boil and thickens. Stir at least twice during cooking.

▶ Stir in salt, pepper and dill. Drain excess water off kohlrabi and pour sauce over. If necessary, reheat until warm for serving.

Makes 4 to 6 servings

TIP To roast chestnuts, cut an X on the flat side of each chestnut, cutting right through to the meat. Spread on plate and microwave at Medium (50%) for 1 to 1½ minutes per dozen, or until soft when squeezed.

Sweet and Sour Beets

Even people who do not love beets will like this dish. Cooking the beets whole in the microwave saves substantial cooking time. Try to buy beets that are the same size, for even cooking.

1 lb	beets (3 to 5 medium)	500 g
¼ cup	water	50 mL
1 tbsp	vegetable oil	15 mL
1	onion, chopped	1
1	clove garlic, minced	1
2 tbsp	brown sugar	25 mL
2 tbsp	white wine vinegar	25 mL
½ tsp	dry mustard	2 mL
½ tsp	horseradish	2 mL
	Salt and freshly ground black pepper to taste	

▶ Trim stem ends and tops off beets. Pierce in several places. Place in a 6 cup (1.5 L) round microwavable casserole with water. Cover and microwave at High (100%) for 10 to 14 minutes, or until beets are tender when pierced with a knife.

▶ Let stand, uncovered, until cool enough to handle, then drain, peel, slice and reserve.

▶ In the same casserole, combine oil, onion and garlic. Microwave, uncovered, at High (100%) for 2 to 4 minutes, or until onion is soft. Stir partway through cooking.

▶ Stir in brown sugar until dissolved. Add vinegar, dry mustard and horseradish and blend. Stir in beets, coating well with mixture. Cover and microwave at High (100%) for 2 to 4 minutes, or until hot. Season to taste with salt and pepper.

Makes 4 servings

TIP Precook potatoes for pan frying or roasting. Pierce potatoes with a knife and cook at High (100%) for 4 minutes for 2 medium potatoes. Then peel, slice or dice for sautéing or roasting.

Gingered Parsnips

Parsnips are a favorite vegetable for many. They are naturally sweet and easily available in the winter when most vegetables on the market have traveled many miles—and taste like it.

1 lb	parsnips (4 to 5 medium)	500 g
2 tbsp	butter	25 mL
1 tbsp	brown sugar or honey	15 mL
	Grated rind and juice of ½ orange, or 2 tbsp (25 mL) frozen orange juice concentrate	
1 tsp	grated fresh ginger	5 mL
	Salt and freshly ground black pepper to taste	

▶ Peel parsnips and cut into julienne strips, discarding woody cores.
▶ In a 6 cup (1.5 L) microwavable casserole, melt butter at High (100%) for 20 to 30 seconds. Stir in brown sugar or honey, orange rind, juice and ginger. Microwave at High (100%) for 20 to 30 seconds, or until sugar is dissolved. Stir well.
▶ Add parsnips and toss to coat evenly. Cover with casserole lid or plastic wrap and microwave at High (100%) for 5 to 7 minutes, or until parsnips are tender and evenly colored. Stir at least once halfway through cooking. Season to taste with salt and pepper. Let stand for 5 minutes before serving.

Makes 4 servings

New Potatoes and Onions

This is a simple but wonderful recipe. Make sure that you use new potatoes no larger than 2½ inches (6 cm) in diameter.

1 tbsp	vegetable oil	15 mL
6	small new potatoes, scrubbed and cut in half	6
1	onion, cut into eighths	1

1 tbsp	butter	15 mL
	Salt and freshly ground black pepper to taste	

▶ In an 8 cup (2 L) microwavable casserole, heat oil at High (100%) for 1½ to 2 minutes, or until hot.
▶ Add potatoes and onion and toss well to coat with oil. Cover and microwave at High (100%) for 6 to 8 minutes, or until potatoes are tender. Shake or stir twice during cooking.
▶ Add butter, salt and pepper to taste, cover and let stand for 5 minutes before serving.

Makes 4 to 6 servings

Sweet Potato Ring

A smooth baked puree with a rich sherry flavor.
This dish can be prepared ahead and refrigerated.
Cook as directed just before serving.

2 lb	sweet potatoes	1 kg
2	eggs	2
¼ cup	cream	50 mL
2 tbsp	butter	25 mL
¼ cup	dry sherry	50 mL
½ tsp	salt	2 mL
¼ tsp	freshly ground black pepper	1 mL
¼ cup	pecan halves	50 mL

▶ Scrub sweet potatoes and pierce skin. Place on paper towel in circular formation in microwave. Microwave at High (100%) for 8 to 12 minutes, or until tender. Let stand 10 minutes.
▶ Peel potatoes while still warm. Mash and beat in eggs, cream, butter, sherry and seasonings, until mixture is smooth. Stir in pecans.
▶ Grease a 6 cup (1.5 L) microwavable ring mold. Spoon potato mixture into mold. Cover with waxed paper.
▶ Microwave at Medium-High (70%) for 7 to 9 minutes, or until set when tested with a toothpick. Let stand, covered, for 5 to 10 minutes. Unmold onto serving plate and serve.

Makes 6 to 8 servings

Potatoes Gratiné

This dish is a quick, updated version of scalloped potatoes.

1½ lb	potatoes (about 4 medium)	750 g
¼ tsp	salt	1 mL
¼ tsp	freshly ground black pepper	1 mL
¼ tsp	ground nutmeg	1 mL
1 cup	sour cream	250 mL
½ cup	grated Swiss cheese	125 mL
pinch	paprika	pinch

▶ Peel and thinly slice potatoes. Layer in an 8 inch (20 cm) round broiler-proof microwavable dish. Sprinkle each layer with a pinch each of salt, pepper and nutmeg.
▶ Cover with waxed paper and microwave at High (100%) for 6 to 10 minutes, or until potatoes are tender. Let stand 2 minutes.
▶ Spread sour cream evenly over potatoes. Cover and microwave at Medium-High (70%) for 2 minutes.
▶ Sprinkle evenly with Swiss cheese and paprika and run under a preheated broiler for 2 to 3 minutes, or until lightly browned. Or microwave, uncovered, at Medium-High (70%) for 1 minute.

Makes 4 to 6 servings

Glazed Mélange of Vegetables

An excellent dish when there are small quantities of several vegetables in the crisper, but not enough of one to serve several people. Use a variety of vegetables to make a colorful dish.

¼ cup	butter	50 mL
2 tbsp	brown sugar	25 mL
4 cups	mixed vegetables—thinly sliced carrots and green beans, slivered onions and green pepper, julienned zucchini, cauliflower cut in florets	1 L
	Grated rind of ½ lemon	

▶ In an 8 cup (2 L) microwavable casserole, combine butter and sugar. Microwave, uncovered, at High (100%) for 2 to 3 minutes, or until butter melts and sugar is dissolved. Stir once during cooking time.

▶ Stir in carrots and onions, tossing to coat with butter-sugar mixture. Cover and microwave at High (100%) for 3 minutes.

▶ Stir in remaining vegetables. Cover and microwave at High (100%) for 3 to 5 minutes, or until vegetables are tender. Stir in grated lemon rind and let stand for a few minutes before serving.

Makes 4 to 6 servings

Vegetable Stir-Fry

Combine your favorite vegetables or use up leftover uncooked vegetables in this slightly sweet stir-fry.

1	onion, sliced	1
4 cups	mixed vegetables—coarsely grated carrots, slivered red or green pepper, julienned zucchini, sliced green or wax beans or snow peas	1 L
1 tbsp	sesame or olive oil	15 mL
1 tsp	grated fresh ginger	5 mL
1 tbsp	rice vinegar	15 mL
1 tsp	soy sauce	5 mL

▶ In an 8 cup (2 L) microwavable casserole, combine onion, carrots, oil and ginger. Microwave, uncovered, at High (100%) for 2 minutes.

▶ Add remaining vegetables and vinegar. Cover and microwave at High (100%) for 6 to 9 minutes, or until vegetables are tender-crisp. Stir twice during cooking. Stir in soy sauce and let stand for a few minutes before serving.

Makes 6 servings

Ratatouille

In order to cook this dish in one step, cut all the vegetables the same size, so they will all need the same cooking time.

8 oz	eggplant, peeled and cut into ¾ inch (2 cm) cubes	250 g
8 oz	zucchini, cut into ¾ inch (2 cm) cubes	250 g
1	green pepper, cut into ¾ inch (2 cm) cubes	1
2	onions, chopped	2
3	ripe tomatoes, peeled, seeded and chopped	3
2	cloves garlic, minced	2
¼ cup	chopped parsley	50 mL
1 tbsp	chopped fresh basil, or 2 tsp (10 mL) dried basil	15 mL
½ tsp	freshly ground black pepper	2 mL
pinch	dried oregano	pinch
2 tbsp	olive oil	25 mL
	Salt to taste	

▶ Combine all ingredients in a 12 cup (3 L) microwavable casserole.
▶ Microwave, uncovered, at High (100%) for 15 to 20 minutes, or until vegetables are tender. Stir three times during cooking. Let stand for 5 minutes.

Makes 4 to 6 servings

9
Sauces

Preparing sauces is a simple joy in the microwave. Sauces to enhance vegetables, main courses or desserts will take mere minutes, without constant stirring, lumps or scorching.

Stock up on glass measures in several sizes—from 1 to 4 cup (250 mL to 1 L) sizes. The round shape is ideal for microwave cooking, and the measuring glasses have the added advantages of a pouring spout and handle. To prevent boilovers, fill the measure only half full.

Although most sauces can be cooked at High (100%), those with delicate ingredients such as eggs or cheese are better cooked on Medium (50%) or Medium-Low (30%) to prevent overcooking and curdling. Stirring with a fork or wire whisk every minute or so will result in smooth, lump-free sauces.

We've included some super sauces, both sweet and savory, to inspire you—including a rich and velvety Béarnaise and easy Hollandaise, as well as decadent chocolate and caramel sauces.

Sauce Tips

▶ A microwavable plastic stirrer or small wooden spoon are ideal, as they can be left in the dish between stirrings. Do not leave metal utensils in the microwave, as they can get hot or arc (page 5).

▶ Most sauces, including delicate Hollandaise, can be reheated beautifully in the microwave. Use a lower power level than you used for cooking, and just heat to serving temperature. (Don't boil, otherwise the sauce may curdle.) Cover to prevent splattering and provide even and gentle heating. If your microwave has a temperature probe, you can use it to reheat a sauce to 140 F (60 C).

▶ Sweet sauces for ice cream can be kept in a heatproof glass jar in the refrigerator. To heat, remove the metal cap and heat briefly at High (100%) until warm. The heating time will depend on the amount.

▶ To make an old-fashioned parfait, prepare a sweet sauce of your choice and let cool slightly. Alternate layers of sauce and softened ice cream in tall serving glasses, then freeze until ready to serve.

▶ Have a super sundae party. Make up lots of dessert sauces, provide different-flavored ice creams and bananas, cherries, nuts and coconut as toppings.

Béarnaise Sauce

This velvety sauce is so easy to prepare in the microwave, that you will probably find yourself making it often. Use it to dress up a plain grilled steak, roast beef or baked potatoes.
To reheat the sauce, add 1 tsp (5 mL) hot water, beat vigorously and microwave at Medium (50%) for 1 to 1½ minutes, or until warm. Do not allow the sauce to boil.

2 tbsp	white or red wine vinegar	25 mL
¼ cup	dry white wine or vermouth	50 mL
2	shallots, minced	2
2 tbsp	chopped fresh tarragon leaves, or 2 tsp (10 mL) dried tarragon	25 mL
3	egg yolks	3
⅓ cup	butter	75 mL
	Salt and freshly ground black pepper to taste	

▶ In a 1 cup (250 mL) glass measure, combine vinegar, wine, shallots and tarragon. Microwave, uncovered, at High (100%) for 2 to 3 minutes, or until boiling. Then microwave for 1 minute longer. Set aside to cool to lukewarm.

▶ Strain sauce into a small bowl and stir in egg yolks.

▶ In a 1 cup (250 mL) glass measure, microwave butter at Medium (50%) for 40 to 60 seconds, or until melted but not boiling. (If butter boils, allow it to cool slightly.)

▶ Vigorously stir egg yolk mixture into butter with a fork or small whisk. Microwave, uncovered, at Medium (50%) for 30 to 90 seconds, stirring every 15 seconds. Cook only until mixture starts to thicken. Season to taste with salt and pepper.

Makes ¾ cup (175 mL)

TIP Recipes that call for a double boiler, such as sauces and pie fillings, can be successfully adapted to microwave cooking. Follow the recipe to combine ingredients, but use a round microwavable casserole and microwave, uncovered, at Medium (50%) or Medium-Low (30%) until thickened, stirring with a whisk every 2 minutes.

Béchamel Sauce

A basic white sauce is a must in every cook's repertoire. When cooked in the microwave, it's not only fast and easy, but you don't have to worry about scorching or messy pots to clean.

2 tbsp	butter	25 mL
2 tbsp	all-purpose flour	25 mL
1 cup	milk	250 mL
¼ tsp	salt	1 mL
¼ tsp	freshly ground black or white pepper	1 mL

▶ Place butter and flour in a 4 cup (1 L) glass measure and microwave, uncovered, at High (100%) for 1½ to 2 minutes, or until butter melts and mixture is bubbly. Stir partway through cooking, so mixture is smooth.

▶ Gradually stir in milk with a wire whisk or fork until smooth. Microwave, uncovered, at High (100%) for 3 to 5 minutes, or until mixture comes to a boil and thickens. Stir partway through cooking. Stir in salt and pepper.

Makes 1 cup (250 mL)

VARIATIONS

Cheese Sauce: Add ¾ cup (175 mL) grated cheese to warm white sauce and stir until melted. If necessary, heat at Medium (50%) for 30 to 60 seconds to help melt cheese. Toss sauce with cooked pasta, or spoon over vegetables or toast.

Dill Sauce: Stir 1 tsp (5 mL) lemon juice and 1 tbsp (15 mL) chopped fresh dill or 1 tsp (5 mL) dried dill weed into warm white sauce. Serve with fish or shellfish.

Horseradish Sauce: Add 1 to 2 tbsp (15 to 25 mL) horseradish to warm white sauce. Good with beef or veal.

Egg Sauce: Add 1 chopped hard-cooked egg and 1 tbsp (15 mL) finely chopped parsley to warm white sauce. Serve with fish or vegetables.

Velouté Sauce: Follow directions for basic white sauce, replacing milk with chicken, fish or beef stock, depending on what the sauce will be served with.

Wine Sauce: Stir 1 to 2 tbsp (15 to 25 mL) white wine, vermouth, port, sherry or Madeira into velouté sauce, along with the stock.

Mornay Sauce: Add 2 tbsp (25 mL) each grated Swiss and Parmesan cheese to white or velouté sauce, and stir until melted. Heat at Medium (50%) to melt cheese if necessary. Good with fish, seafood, ham or vegetables.

Curry Sauce

A good recipe to have tucked away when a fast meal is in order. Add cooked ham, pork, lamb or beef and serve with cooked rice or noodles and a tossed salad.

1	onion, chopped	1
½	green or red pepper, or 1 stalk celery, chopped	½
3 tbsp	butter	50 mL
3 tbsp	all-purpose flour	50 mL
1 to 2 tsp	curry powder	5 to 10 mL
½ tsp	ground cumin	2 mL
pinch	salt	pinch
pinch	granulated sugar	pinch
pinch	freshly ground black pepper	pinch
1½ cups	beef or chicken stock	375 mL

▶ In a 4 cup (1 L) glass measure, combine onion, pepper or celery and butter. Microwave, uncovered, at High (100%) for 2 to 3 minutes, or until vegetables are softened. Stir partway through cooking.
▶ Stir in flour and seasonings, blending well. Microwave, uncovered, at High (100%) for 30 seconds.
▶ Whisk in stock until smooth. Microwave, uncovered, at High (100%) for 3 to 4 minutes, or until sauce comes to a boil and thickens.

Makes 2 cups (500 mL)

Barbecue Sauce

This sauce has a real barbecue flavor. And if you use a food processor, it will be even easier to prepare. If you like, stir in a shot of Bourbon at the end. This sauce keeps for about one month in the refrigerator; it also freezes well.

1 cup	chopped onion	250 mL
½ cup	chopped celery	125 mL
2 tbsp	vinegar	25 mL
2 tbsp	brown sugar	25 mL
1 cup	ketchup	250 mL
2 tbsp	Worcestershire sauce	25 mL
¼ tsp	dry mustard	1 mL
pinch	cayenne	pinch
¼ cup	water	50 mL
2 tbsp	Bourbon, optional	25 mL

▶ Combine all ingredients except Bourbon in an 8 cup (2 L) microwavable bowl or glass measure. Cover with waxed paper. Microwave at High (100%) for 8 to 10 minutes, or until sauce comes to a boil and thickens. Stir twice during cooking.
▶ Stir in Bourbon if desired.

Makes 2 cups (500 mL)

Hollandaise Sauce

Rich and delicious, Hollandaise sauce is a must for poached fish and steamed artichokes (page 30). Making Hollandaise requires attention and vigorous whisking to redistribute the heat on the outer edges of the dish.

½ cup	butter	125 mL
3 tbsp	fresh lemon juice	50 mL
pinch	dry mustard	pinch
pinch	cayenne	pinch
3	egg yolks, lightly beaten	3

▶ In a 2 cup (500 mL) microwavable bowl, melt butter at High (100%) for 40 to 60 seconds. Do not let butter get too hot, or sauce may curdle.

▶ Whisk lemon juice, dry mustard and cayenne into butter. (This will help cool butter slightly.)

▶ Whisk egg yolks into butter. Microwave, uncovered, at Medium-Low (30%) for 1 to 3 minutes, until sauce thickens and is creamy. Whisk every 30 seconds during cooking time. If sauce is overcooked, it will separate. If this happens, whisk 1 to 2 tbsp (15 to 25 mL) ice-cold water into sauce until it returns to a creamy consistency.

Makes ½ cup (125 mL)

Sweet and Sour Sauce

A delicious and easy sauce. Make mini meatballs and serve with this sauce as an appetizer, or add cooked chicken, beef or pork for a quick meal.

1	19 oz (540 mL) can unsweetened pineapple chunks	1
½ cup	white wine vinegar	125 mL
½ cup	lightly packed brown sugar	125 mL
¼ cup	ketchup	50 mL
1 tbsp	soy sauce	15 mL
1 tbsp	cornstarch	15 mL
2 tbsp	water	25 mL

▶ Drain pineapple juice into a 4 cup (1 L) glass measure, reserving pineapple chunks. Blend in vinegar, brown sugar, ketchup and soy sauce. Microwave, uncovered, at High (100%) for 4 to 6 minutes, or until sauce comes to a boil. Stir partway through cooking.

▶ In a small bowl or cup, combine cornstarch and water until smooth. Add about ¼ cup (50 mL) hot sauce to cornstarch mixture until blended. Stir back into sauce and microwave, uncovered, at High (100%) for 1 to 2 minutes, or until sauce boils and thickens. Stir in pineapple chunks.

Makes 3 cups (750 mL)

Creamy Salad Dressing

A delicious and easy salad dressing to have on hand. It will keep for up to two months in the refrigerator. Use it in sandwiches instead of mayonnaise.

2 tbsp	all-purpose flour	25 mL
2 tbsp	granulated sugar	25 mL
⅔ cup	milk or cream	150 mL
2	eggs, lightly beaten	2
½ tsp	dry mustard	2 mL
¼ tsp	salt	1 mL
pinch	cayenne	pinch
¼ cup	lemon juice or vinegar	50 mL

▶ In a 2 cup (500 mL) glass measure or microwavable bowl, combine flour and sugar. Whisk in milk or cream until smooth.

▶ Microwave, uncovered, at High (100%) for 1 to 1½ minutes, or until hot but not boiling. Stir well, add eggs and beat until smooth.

▶ Microwave, uncovered, at Medium (50%) for 2 to 3 minutes, or until thickened. Stir twice during cooking. Whisk in dry mustard, salt, cayenne and lemon juice. Refrigerate immediately in a covered container.

Makes 1 cup (250 mL)

VARIATIONS
Blue Cheese Dressing: Stir ¼ cup (50 mL) crumbled blue cheese, Roquefort or Stilton into the cooled dressing.

Potato Salad Dressing: To cooled dressing, add ¼ cup (50 mL) sour cream, 1 tbsp (15 mL) Hot and Sweet Mustard (page 183) or ½ tsp (2 mL) dry mustard.

Fruit Dressing: Beat ½ cup (125 mL) plain yogurt or sour cream, 1 tbsp (15 mL) honey and ¼ cup (50 mL) strawberry, peach or blueberry jam into cooled dressing. Spoon over diced fruit and toss for a summer fruit salad.

Rich Chocolate Sauce

A rich, decadent sauce that's wonderful over ice cream. It keeps well, so make it ahead of time. Keep it in the refrigerator and reheat before serving.

3 oz	unsweetened chocolate	90 g
½ cup	milk	125 mL
¾ to 1 cup	granulated sugar	175 to 250 mL
¼ cup	butter	50 mL
1 tsp	vanilla	5 mL

▶ Combine chocolate and milk in a 4 cup (1 L) glass measure. Microwave, uncovered, at High (100%) for 2 to 3 minutes, or until chocolate melts. Stir once or twice during cooking.
▶ Stir in sugar until dissolved. (It may be necessary to microwave at High (100%) for 30 to 60 seconds to dissolve sugar completely.)
▶ Stir in butter until melted. Add vanilla and serve warm over ice cream. Store any leftover sauce in a covered jar in refrigerator.

Makes 1½ cups (375 mL)

VARIATIONS

Rum Sauce: Stir 1 to 2 tbsp (15 to 25 mL) rum into warm sauce.

Chocolate Mint Sauce: Add 1 to 1½ tsp (5 to 7 mL) peppermint extract to sauce with vanilla.

Mocha Sauce: Stir 1 tsp (5 mL) instant coffee into warm sauce until dissolved.

TIP To soften ice cream for easier scooping, heat 4 cups (1 L) ice cream for 10 to 20 seconds at High (100%).

TIP Warm ice cream toppings or maple syrup—remove the metal cap and microwave at High (100%) for 30 seconds per ½ cup (125 mL).

Cranberry Orange Sauce

So easy and quick to make to accompany your Christmas or Thanksgiving turkey. The orange gives the sauce a nice sharpness.

12 oz	fresh cranberries	340 g
1½ cups	granulated sugar	375 mL
¼ cup	water	50 mL
	Grated rind and juice of 1 orange	
1 tbsp	Cointreau, Grand Marnier or Triple Sec	15 mL

▶ Wash and pick over cranberries, discarding stems and unripe fruit.

▶ In an 8 cup (2 L) glass measure or microwavable casserole, combine cranberries, sugar, water, orange rind and juice. Microwave, uncovered, at High (100%) for 6 to 9 minutes, or until cranberries pop and soften. Stir once during cooking.

▶ Stir well to crush berries. Add liqueur. Taste and add more sugar, if desired. Store any leftover sauce in a covered jar in refrigerator.

Makes 3 cups (750 mL)

Strawberry Orange Sauce

Delicious with crêpes, over ice cream or over a white or lemon cake. As a variation, substitute raspberries or blueberries for the strawberries. For a nice touch, add 1 tbsp (15 mL) orange liqueur to the sauce with the lemon juice.

½ cup	granulated sugar	125 mL
2 tbsp	cornstarch	25 mL
1 cup	unsweetened orange juice	250 mL
1 cup	sliced strawberries	250 mL
1 tbsp	lemon juice	15 mL

▶ Combine sugar, cornstarch and orange juice in a 4 cup (1 L) glass measure, stirring until smooth. Add strawberries.

▶ Microwave, uncovered, at High (100%) for 4 to 5 minutes, or until sauce comes to a boil and thickens. Stir partway through cooking.
▶ Stir in lemon juice. Store any leftover sauce in a covered jar in refrigerator.

Makes 1½ cups (375 mL)

Peanut Butter Fudge Sauce

Peanut butter and chocolate—what a wonderful combination! Children and peanut-butter fans of all ages will love this rich sauce.

6 oz	semisweet or bittersweet chocolate	180 g
¼ cup	granulated sugar	50 mL
¾ cup	milk	175 mL
½ cup	smooth peanut butter	125 mL

▶ Combine chocolate, sugar and milk in a 4 cup (1 L) glass measure. Microwave, uncovered, at High (100%) for 2 to 3 minutes, until sauce comes to a boil. Stir partway through cooking.
▶ Stir in peanut butter and microwave at High (100%) for 30 to 60 seconds, or until peanut butter is melted. Stir until smooth. Serve warm or cool over ice cream. Store any leftover sauce in a covered jar in refrigerator.

Makes 1½ cups (375 mL)

TIP To soften butter, cream cheese or peanut butter, remove wrapper or metal cap and microwave ½ cup (125 mL) at Medium-Low (30%) for 10 to 15 seconds.

Old-fashioned Nutmeg Sauce

An easy sauce to go with a carrot or plum pudding (pages 154 and 156). You can make this sauce ahead of time, as it keeps well and reheats easily.

⅓ cup	brown sugar	75 mL
1 tbsp	cornstarch	15 mL
⅔ cup	water	150 mL
2 tbsp	butter	25 mL
1 tsp	vanilla	5 mL
pinch	ground nutmeg	pinch

▶ In a 2 cup (500 mL) glass measure, combine brown sugar and cornstarch. Gradually stir in water until smooth.
▶ Microwave, uncovered, at High (100%) for 1½ to 2 minutes, or until mixture comes to a boil and thickens. Stir partway through cooking.
▶ Stir in butter until melted. Cool slightly and add vanilla and nutmeg. Serve warm over pudding. Or cool, cover and refrigerate. Just before serving, reheat at High (100%) for 1 minute, or until heated through.

Makes ¾ cup (175 mL)

Caramel Sauce

Be sure to use a heavy glass container for making the caramel, and watch carefully to avoid burning.

1 cup	granulated sugar	250 mL
⅓ cup	water	75 mL
1 cup	whipping cream	250 mL
2 tbsp	butter	25 mL
½ tsp	vanilla	2 mL

▶ In a heavy 4 cup (1 L) glass measure or casserole, blend sugar and water. Microwave at High (100%) for 8 to 10 minutes, or until mixture is a rich caramel color (about the color of maple syrup).

▶ Remove from microwave and place on a heatproof trivet or countertop (if placed on a cold surface, glass may break). Carefully pour in cream (the mixture will boil up) and stir with a wooden spoon until smooth.

▶ Stir in butter until melted, then stir in vanilla. The sauce will thicken as it cools. Store in a covered glass jar in the refrigerator.

▶ To serve, remove lid and heat at High (100%) until warm. Serve over ice cream.

Makes 2 cups (500 mL)

Lemon Sauce

This sauce is ideal for dressing up a plain cake or gingerbread.

½ cup	granulated sugar	125 mL
1 tbsp	cornstarch	15 mL
¾ cup	water	175 mL
	Grated rind and juice of 1 lemon	
2 tbsp	butter	25 mL

▶ In a 2 cup (500 mL) glass measure, combine sugar and cornstarch. Gradually stir in water until smooth. Add grated lemon rind.

▶ Microwave, uncovered, at High (100%) for 2 to 3 minutes, or until mixture comes to a boil and thickens. Stir partway through cooking.

▶ Add lemon juice and butter and stir until butter melts. Serve sauce warm or cold. Store any leftover sauce in a covered jar in refrigerator.

Makes 1¼ cups (300 mL)

VARIATION
Orange Sauce: Substitute grated rind and juice of 1 orange for the lemon, and cook as above.

Crème Anglaise

Also known as vanilla custard sauce, this smooth, rich sauce can transform fresh fruit into a special dessert, or be used in trifles or other desserts. It can also be used as the base for homemade vanilla ice cream. If you are not using the sauce immediately, cover it with buttered waxed paper or plastic wrap to prevent a skin from forming on the surface.

⅓ cup	granulated sugar	75 mL
2 tbsp	cornstarch	25 mL
1½ cups	milk	375 mL
2	eggs	2
1 tsp	vanilla	5 mL

▶ In a 4 cup (1 L) glass measure, combine sugar and cornstarch. Stir in milk until smooth.
▶ Microwave, uncovered, at High (100%) for 4 to 6 minutes, or until mixture comes to a boil and thickens. Stir twice during cooking.
▶ In a small bowl or cup, lightly beat eggs. Add a small amount of the hot milk mixture to the eggs. Pour the warmed eggs back into the milk mixture, stirring constantly.
▶ Microwave at Medium (50%) for 1 minute. Stir. The sauce should be smooth and thick. Stir in vanilla.

Makes 2 cups (500 mL)

VARIATION
Chocolate Custard Sauce: Add 2 tbsp (25 mL) cocoa to the cornstarch mixture, and increase sugar to ⅔ cup (150 mL).

TIP Scald milk for custards, hot chocolate or when making yogurt—1 cup (250 mL) will require 2 to 3 minutes at High (100%).

10
Cakes and Squares

We've encountered so many people who say you can't bake in a microwave oven, that we feel obligated to prove differently. Not only can you bake, but steam puddings, make sinfully rich cheesecakes, delicious squares and bars with a minimum of fuss.

We know few people who don't like to indulge in desserts, but with less time to spend preparing and cooking these days, not many make the effort to bake, except when company's coming. With the microwave, you can generally bake a cake in ten minutes—less time than it takes to preheat some conventional ovens.

Steamed puddings are a natural for the moist cooking method of the microwave. They steam in ten minutes rather than four to eight hours. Because of the density of the batter, a ring mold is the best shape, or use custard cups if you prefer individual puddings. Otherwise, you'll have difficulty getting the center cooked through. Steamed puddings also reheat easily.

You will quickly see the cooking pattern of your microwave oven when baking. It may be necessary to rotate cakes, squares and cheesecakes at least once during cooking. Some cakes are improved when elevated on a microwave roasting rack or inverted saucer when cooking.

Baking Tips

▶ Round or ring-shaped baking dishes, particularly clear glass ones, produce the most even baking and are the easiest to check for doneness. Dense quickbreads and steamed puddings are best baked in ring shapes as the microwave energy penetrates from all sides of the ring and eliminates the problem of an undercooked center.

▶ Line layer cake dishes with waxed or parchment paper, if the cake is to be turned out. Lightly butter ring molds, but do not flour dishes, as this leaves an unattractive film on the cake.

▶ For bar cookies, squares and brownies, baking dishes require no greasing or preparation.

▶ Microwave cakes rise higher than cakes baked in a conventional oven, so fill baking dishes only half full.

▶ Bake cakes and bar cookies uncovered. Steamed puddings should be covered.

▶ Starting cakes at Medium (50%) power produces a good texture, a smoother surface and more even baking. Finish at High (100%) to complete baking.

▶ Check doneness at the minimum cooking time given in a recipe. Cakes will be done when a toothpick inserted in several places comes out clean, and when most of the moistness disappears from the top. Touch moist spots on top of cake with your finger—if the cake underneath is dry, it's done.

▶ Let cake, cheesecake or squares stand directly on a counter or wooden board, rather than on a rack, to cool. This helps distribute the heat during the standing time. Let stand for 10 minutes before removing from dish.

Apricot Almond Pudding

This is a lovely steamed pudding that's not too sweet. Use a fancy, fluted ceramic ring mold for an attractive presentation. If you do not have a ring mold, use a 4 cup (1 L) round casserole or bowl with a juice glass placed in the center.

⅓ cup	butter	75 mL
¼ cup	granulated sugar	50 mL
2	eggs	2
¼ tsp	almond extract	1 mL
½ cup	all-purpose flour	125 mL
1 tsp	baking powder	5 mL
⅓ cup	ground almonds	75 mL
2 tbsp	milk	25 mL
12	dried apricots, chopped	12

▶ Lightly butter a 4 cup (1 L) microwavable ring mold.

▶ In medium bowl, beat butter and sugar together until smooth. Add eggs and almond extract and beat until lemony in color.

▶ In separate bowl, combine flour, baking powder and ground almonds. Add to egg mixture along with milk and apricots and stir until smooth. Pour into buttered mold.

▶ Cover with plastic wrap or lid and microwave at Medium (50%) for 5 to 7 minutes, or until a toothpick inserted in several places comes out clean. Rotate dish, if necessary, during cooking.

▶ Let stand, uncovered, for 5 minutes. Unmold and cut in wedges.

▶ Serve warm with Crème Anglaise (page 142), whipped cream or plain yogurt.

Makes 6 servings

Chocolate Cointreau Cake

This chocolate cake is dense, moist and very rich. Grand Marnier or any other orange liqueur can be substituted for the Cointreau. You can garnish this cake with Candied Fruit Peel (page 186) or white chocolate leaves (page 179).

3 oz	good-quality bittersweet or semisweet chocolate	90 g
¾ cup	all-purpose flour	175 mL
½ tsp	baking powder	2 mL
½ tsp	baking soda	2 mL
¼ tsp	salt	1 mL
½ cup	butter, softened	125 mL
½ cup	granulated sugar	125 mL
2	eggs	2
½ tsp	vanilla	2 mL
	Grated rind of 1 orange	
1 tbsp	Cointreau	15 mL
½ cup	sour cream	125 mL
CHOCOLATE FROSTING		
4 oz	good-quality bittersweet or semisweet chocolate	125 g
2 tbsp	butter, softened	25 mL
½ cup	sifted icing sugar	125 mL
1 tbsp	Cointreau	15 mL
1 to 2 tbsp	milk	15 to 25 mL

▶ Line bottom of 9 inch (23 cm) round glass baking dish with a circle of waxed paper.

▶ Melt chocolate in small microwavable dish at Medium (50%) for 3 to 4 minutes. Stir occasionally to help chocolate melt. Set aside.

▶ In bowl, combine flour, baking powder, baking soda and salt. Set aside.

▶ In large bowl, cream butter, then add granulated sugar and beat until light and fluffy. Add eggs, one at a time, then vanilla, orange rind and Cointreau. Beat until light. Stir in cooled melted chocolate.

▶ Add dry ingredients alternately with sour cream, beginning and ending with dry ingredients. Beat well after each addition.

► Spoon batter into baking dish and smooth out. Microwave, uncovered, at Medium (50%) for 4 minutes. Rotate dish, if necessary, and microwave at High (100%) for 3 to 6 minutes, or until toothpick inserted in several places comes out clean. Let stand on countertop for 10 to 15 minutes to cool.

► Invert cake onto serving plate. Remove waxed paper and let cool completely before frosting.

► To make frosting, melt chocolate in microwavable bowl, at Medium (50%) for 3 to 4 minutes. Stir occasionally to help melt chocolate.

► Beat in butter until smooth. Beat in icing sugar, then Cointreau and just enough milk to make a spreading consistency. Spread over cooled cake.

Makes 8 to 10 servings

TIP   For more flavor, warm roasted coffee beans before grinding. Spread out on a microwavable plate and microwave briefly at High (100%) just until warmed and fragrant.

TIP   To warm brandy or liqueurs for flaming, microwave ¼ cup (50 mL) at High (100%) for about 20 seconds.

Orange Carrot Cake

A moist cake such as a carrot cake is superb when baked in the microwave. The grated orange rind makes this one especially delicious.

½ cup	vegetable oil	125 mL
¾ cup	granulated sugar	175 mL
2	eggs	2
1 cup	grated raw carrot, about 2 medium	250 mL
½ cup	raisins	125 mL
	Grated rind and juice of 1 orange	
1 cup	all-purpose flour	250 mL
1 tsp	baking powder	5 mL
1 tsp	cinnamon	5 mL
½ tsp	baking soda	2 mL
¼ tsp	salt	1 mL
¼ tsp	ground nutmeg	1 mL

CREAM CHEESE FROSTING

4 oz	cream cheese, softened	125 g
2 tbsp	butter, softened	25 mL
2 tbsp	grated orange rind	25 mL
½ tsp	vanilla	2 mL
1½ cups	sifted icing sugar	375 mL

▶ Blend oil and sugar in a large bowl. Beat in eggs one at a time. Stir in carrot, raisins, orange rind and juice.

▶ In separate bowl, combine dry ingredients. Stir into carrot mixture just until blended.

▶ Pour into a 9 inch (23 cm) round glass baking dish lined with a circle of waxed paper. Microwave, uncovered, at Medium (50%) for 4 minutes. Rotate dish, if necessary, and microwave at High (100%) for 3 to 5 minutes, or until a toothpick inserted in several places comes out clean.

▶ Let stand on counter for 10 to 15 minutes. Turn cake out onto a serving plate. Remove waxed paper and cool completely.

▶ To make frosting, combine cream cheese and butter and beat to blend. Stir in orange rind and vanilla, then beat in icing sugar until smooth. Spread on cooled cake.

Makes 8 to 10 servings

Amaretto Cheesecake with Raspberry Sauce

Cheesecakes are best made ahead and chilled. This one has a delicious almond flavor with an interesting almond base that cuts easily. It is served on top of a raspberry sauce.

¼ cup	butter	50 mL
2 cups	chopped almonds	500 mL
2 tbsp	granulated sugar	25 mL
12 oz	cream cheese, softened	375 g
½ cup	granulated sugar	125 mL
3	eggs	3
1 cup	sour cream	250 mL
¼ cup	Amaretto	50 mL
½ tsp	vanilla	2 mL
½ tsp	almond extract	2 mL
3 cups	fresh raspberries or strawberries	750 mL

▶ In 9 inch (23 cm) microwavable quiche dish, deep pie plate or round baking dish, melt butter at High (100%) for 1 to 1½ minutes.
▶ Stir in almonds (a food processor works well to chop nuts to an even consistency) and 2 tbsp (25 mL) sugar until evenly coated with butter. Press onto bottom and sides of dish. Microwave at High (100%) for 2 to 3 minutes, or until firm. Set aside.
▶ In large bowl, beat cream cheese and sugar until light. Beat in eggs one at a time. Add sour cream, 2 tbsp (25 mL) Amaretto, vanilla and almond extract. Beat until smooth.
▶ Pour into baked crust. Microwave, uncovered, at Medium (50%) for 14 to 18 minutes, or until cheesecake is just set in the center. Rotate dish partway through cooking, if necessary.
▶ Cool to room temperature, then cover and refrigerate until serving time.
▶ Just before serving, puree raspberries, then sieve to remove seeds. Add remaining Amaretto. Taste and add sugar if necessary.
▶ To serve, spoon some of raspberry sauce on dessert plates. Place a slice of cheesecake on top of sauce.

Makes 8 servings

Chocolate Swirl Cheesecake

Make early in the day or the day before to completely chill before serving.

¼ cup	butter	50 mL
1¼ cups	chocolate wafer crumbs or chocolate Graham cracker crumbs	300 mL
2 tbsp	granulated sugar	25 mL
2 oz	semisweet chocolate	60 g
12 oz	cream cheese, softened	375 g
½ cup	granulated sugar	125 mL
3	eggs	3
1 cup	sour cream	250 mL
1 tsp	vanilla	5 mL

► In a 9 inch (23 cm) microwavable quiche dish, round baking dish or deep pie plate, melt butter at High (100%) for 1 to 1½ minutes. Stir in crumbs and 2 tbsp (25 mL) sugar until evenly coated with butter. Press onto bottom and sides of dish.

► Microwave at High (100%) for 2 to 3 minutes, or until firm. Rotate dish, if necessary, during cooking.

► In a small dish, melt chocolate at Medium (50%) for 2 to 3 minutes, stirring to help chocolate melt. Set aside.

► In large bowl, beat cream cheese and sugar until light. Beat in eggs, one at a time, then add sour cream and vanilla and beat until smooth.

► Pour into baked crust. Drizzle chocolate over mixture in an attractive pattern. Microwave, uncovered, at Medium (50%) for 14 to 18 minutes, or until cheesecake is almost set in the center. Rotate dish during cooking, if necessary.

► Cool on countertop to room temperature, then refrigerate until serving.

Makes 8 servings

Lemon Cheesecake Squares

These light squares make delicious additions to the "brown bags" of young and old alike.

⅓ cup	butter, softened	75 mL
⅓ cup	brown sugar	75 mL
1 cup	all-purpose flour	250 mL
½ cup	finely chopped hazelnuts or almonds	125 mL
8 oz	cream cheese, softened	250 g
¼ cup	granulated sugar	50 mL
1	egg	1
2 tbsp	milk	25 mL
2 tbsp	lemon juice	25 mL
1 tsp	grated lemon rind	5 mL
½ tsp	vanilla	2 mL

▶ In a medium bowl, cream butter and brown sugar until light. Add flour and nuts and stir until mixture is crumbly.

▶ Reserve 1 cup (250 mL) of mixture for topping. Press remainder in bottom of an 8 inch (20 cm) square glass baking dish. Microwave, uncovered, at High (100%) for 2 to 3 minutes, or until firm. Rotate dish, if necessary, partway through cooking. Set aside.

▶ In a medium bowl, beat cream cheese and granulated sugar until smooth. Beat in egg, then remaining ingredients until smooth. Spread evenly over baked crust, then sprinkle with reserved crumb mixture.

▶ Microwave, uncovered, at Medium (50%) for 10 to 12 minutes, or until firm in the center. Rotate dish, if necessary, during cooking.

▶ Let stand until cool, then refrigerate. Cut into 2 inch (5 cm) squares.

Makes 16 squares

TIP   Soften brown sugar by placing 1 cup (250 mL) hard sugar in a dish with a slice of bread or an apple wedge. Cover and microwave at High (100%) for 30 to 60 seconds.

Lemon Coffee Cake

A light, moist cake with a lemon glaze. A variation is a crunchy cinnamon streusel topping. Both are delicious with coffee or tea.

1½ cups	all-purpose flour	375 mL
1½ tsp	baking powder	7 mL
½ tsp	baking soda	2 mL
¼ tsp	salt	1 mL
½ cup	butter, softened	125 mL
½ cup	granulated sugar	125 mL
2	eggs	2
½ tsp	vanilla	2 mL
	Grated rind of 1 lemon	
1 cup	sour cream	250 mL
LEMON GLAZE		
1 tbsp	butter	15 mL
1 cup	icing sugar	250 mL
1 tbsp	grated lemon rind	15 mL
½ tsp	vanilla	2 mL
2 to 3 tbsp	lemon juice	25 to 50 mL

▶ Lightly butter a 6 cup (1.5 L) microwave ring mold.

▶ In medium bowl, combine flour, baking powder, baking soda and salt. Set aside.

▶ In large bowl, cream butter and granulated sugar until light. Beat in eggs, one at a time, then vanilla and lemon rind.

▶ Add dry ingredients to egg mixture alternately with sour cream just until blended. Do not overmix. Batter will be quite thick.

▶ Spoon batter into ring mold. Microwave, uncovered, at Medium (50%) for 6 minutes. Rotate dish, if necessary, and microwave at High (100%) for 2 to 5 minutes, or until toothpick inserted in several places comes out clean. Let stand directly on counter for 10 to 15 minutes. Run a knife along the edges and invert cake. Cool before glazing. .

▶ To make glaze, in a small microwavable bowl, melt butter at High (100%) for 20 to 30 seconds.

▶ Stir in icing sugar, lemon rind and vanilla. Add lemon juice, 1 tbsp (15 mL) at a time, and stir until mixture is a thick, pouring consistency.

Pour over cake. Garnish with additional grated lemon rind or lemon slices.

VARIATION
Streusel Coffee Cake

¼ cup	brown sugar	50 mL
1 tsp	cinnamon	5 mL
¼ cup	finely chopped nuts	50 mL

▶ Combine brown sugar, cinnamon and nuts. Sprinkle half of mixture in the bottom of lightly buttered 6 cup (1.5 L) ring mold. Prepare batter as above and spoon half of batter in ring mold. Sprinkle with remaining topping mixture, then cover with remaining batter.
▶ Microwave as above.

Makes 8 to 10 servings

TIP To shorten the proofing time of bread doughs, place dough in a greased microwavable bowl and cover with waxed paper. Place a 2 cup (500 mL) glass measure containing 1½ cups (375 mL) water in microwave oven and bring to a boil at High (100%). Then place covered bowl of dough in microwave with water and microwave at Low (10%) for 4 minutes. Let stand for 15 minutes. Repeat microwaving and standing until dough is double in bulk. Rotate dish occasionally.

Traditional Carrot Pudding

Steamed puddings are ideal for moist microwave cooking. Instead of steaming in a large pot for 4 to 8 hours, this traditional carrot-suet pudding steams in about 10 minutes, and reheats just as easily. Ground suet is a highly perishable beef fat that can often be found in the frozen food section of supermarkets in the late fall.

1 cup	raisins	250 mL
½ cup	currants	125 mL
1 tbsp	brandy	15 mL
1 cup	ground suet	250 mL
1 cup	dark brown sugar	250 mL
1 cup	grated raw carrot, about 2 medium	250 mL
1 cup	grated raw potato	250 mL
1 cup	all-purpose flour	250 mL
1 tsp	baking soda	5 mL
½ tsp	salt	2 mL
1 tsp	cinnamon	5 mL
½ tsp	ground nutmeg	2 mL
¼ tsp	ground cloves	1 mL

▶ Combine raisins and currants in a small microwavable bowl. Sprinkle with brandy and microwave, uncovered, at High (100%) for 30 seconds to plump up fruit.

▶ In a large bowl, combine suet, sugar, carrots, potato, raisins and currants.

▶ In separate bowl, combine flour, baking soda and seasonings. Stir into carrot-suet mixture until well moistened.

▶ Spoon batter into buttered 6 cup (1.5 L) microwave ring mold. Cover with plastic wrap and microwave at Medium (50%) for 8 minutes. Rotate, if necessary, and microwave at High (100%) for 2 to 4 minutes, or until pudding begins to pull away from edge of dish and toothpick inserted in several places comes out clean. Let stand, uncovered, for 10 to 15 minutes before turning out of dish.

▶ When completely cool, wrap in brandy-soaked cheesecloth, then in plastic wrap. Keep in a cool place.

▶ To serve, reheat, without unwrapping, at Medium (50%) for 4 to 6 minutes, or until warm. Serve with Old-fashioned Nutmeg Sauce (page 140).

Makes 8 to 12 servings

Mocha Pecan Brownies

Although traditional brownies are baked in a square, bar cookies and cakes cook more evenly in a round dish in the microwave. For a wicked dessert, serve a scoop of vanilla ice cream on each brownie wedge and top with Rich Chocolate Sauce (page 137).

2 oz	unsweetened chocolate	60 g
½ cup	butter	125 mL
1 tbsp	instant coffee powder	15 mL
1 cup	all-purpose flour	250 mL
½ tsp	baking powder	2 mL
½ tsp	salt	2 mL
2	eggs	2
1 cup	granulated sugar	250 mL
1 tsp	vanilla	5 mL
1 cup	chopped pecans	250 mL
FROSTING		
2 oz	bittersweet or semisweet chocolate	60 g
2 tbsp	butter	25 mL

▶ Combine unsweetened chocolate and butter in a small microwavable dish. Microwave at High (100%) for 1 to 2 minutes, or until melted. Stir to help chocolate melt. Stir in instant coffee until dissolved and set aside to cool.

▶ In small bowl, combine flour, baking powder and salt. Set aside.

▶ In a medium bowl, beat eggs until light. Gradually beat in sugar, then vanilla. Stir in cooled chocolate mixture until evenly blended.

▶ Add flour mixture and stir just until blended, then fold in pecans. Spoon batter into a round 9 inch (23 cm) glass baking dish.

▶ Microwave, uncovered, at High (100%) for 4 to 6 minutes, or until toothpick inserted in several places comes out clean. Rotate dish, if necessary, partway through cooking. Let stand directly on counter top until cool.

▶ To make frosting, combine chocolate and butter in a small microwavable bowl and microwave, uncovered, at High (100%) for 1 to 1½ minutes, or until melted. Stir well to blend. Pour over cooled brownies and spread with a knife. Cut into wedges.

Makes 16 servings or more

Plum Pudding

This is a rich steamed pudding filled with fruit, candied peel and cherries. Make it a few weeks ahead. Wrap in brandy-soaked cheesecloth and let mellow in a cool place.
To make smaller puddings for individual servings or as gifts, spoon batter into buttered custard cups. Do not fill more than two-thirds full. Cover and microwave. For half the recipe, reduce cooking time by half. Test with a toothpick inserted in several places and let stand 10 minutes before turning out.

1 cup	dark raisins	250 mL
½ cup	currants	125 mL
½ cup	chopped mixed peel	125 mL
½ cup	halved glace cherries	125 mL
¼ cup	slivered almonds	50 mL
2 tbsp	brandy	25 mL
1	egg	1
½ cup	dark brown sugar	125 mL
½ cup	milk	125 mL
¼ cup	vegetable oil	50 mL
¼ cup	molasses	50 mL
1 cup	all-purpose flour	250 mL
1 cup	soft breadcrumbs	250 mL
1 tsp	baking soda	5 mL
1 tsp	cinnamon	5 mL
½ tsp	salt	2 mL
½ tsp	ground nutmeg	2 mL
¼ tsp	ground cloves	1 mL

▶ Combine raisins, currants, peel, cherries and almonds in a large microwavable bowl. Stir in brandy, cover with vented plastic wrap and microwave at High (100%) for 1 minute. This plumps up the fruit and gives them a better flavor. Set aside.
▶ In a small bowl, lightly beat egg. Stir in sugar, milk, oil and molasses. Set aside.
▶ In a separate bowl, combine remaining dry ingredients.
▶ Stir liquid mixture into fruit mixture until evenly blended. Fold in dry ingredients just until well moistened.
▶ Spoon batter into a buttered 6 cup (1.5 L) microwave ring mold.

Do not fill more than two-thirds full, as batter will rise during cooking. Cover with plastic wrap.

▶ Microwave at Medium (50%) for 8 minutes. Rotate, if necessary, and microwave at High (100%) for 2 to 4 minutes, or until toothpick inserted in several places comes out clean.

▶ Let stand, uncovered, for about 10 minutes. Turn out of dish and cool completely.

▶ To store, wrap in brandy-soaked cheesecloth, then in plastic wrap. Keep in a cool place.

▶ To serve, reheat, without unwrapping, at Medium (50%) for 4 to 6 minutes, or until warm. Serve with warm Old-fashioned Nutmeg Sauce (page 140). To flame pudding, heat 2 tbsp (25 mL) brandy in a 1 cup (250 mL) glass measure at High (100%) for 10 seconds. Pour over warm pudding and quickly ignite.

Makes 8 to 10 servings

TIP To soften honey that has crystallized, remove the metal cap from the jar and heat at High (100%) for 10 to 20 seconds per cup (250 mL).

TIP Plump raisins or currants in the microwave by adding 1 tsp (5 mL) water, juice or brandy per cup (250 mL). Microwave for 15 seconds at High (100%).

Apricot Orange Bars

A quick bar cookie with the goodness of oatmeal. For a change of pace, try a date or fig filling (see below).

2 cups	chopped dried apricots, about 10 oz (300 g)	500 mL
2 tbsp	granulated sugar	25 mL
½ cup	unsweetened orange juice	125 mL
	Grated rind of 1 orange	
1 cup	all-purpose flour	250 mL
¼ tsp	baking powder	1 mL
½ cup	brown sugar	125 mL
1½ cups	rolled oats	375 mL
½ cup	butter, softened	125 mL

▶ Combine apricots, sugar, orange juice and rind in a 4 cup (1 L) glass measure or microwavable casserole. Microwave, uncovered, at High (100%) for 4 to 6 minutes, or until apricots are softened. Stir once during cooking. Set aside.

▶ In a medium bowl, combine flour, baking powder, brown sugar and rolled oats. Stir in softened butter until mixture is crumbly. Press about two-thirds of mixture in bottom of an 8 inch (20 cm) square glass baking dish. Microwave, uncovered, at High (100%) for 2 to 3 minutes, or until firm.

▶ Spread apricot mixture carefully and evenly over base, then top with remaining crumb mixture and pat down.

▶ Microwave, uncovered, at High (100%) for 4 to 6 minutes, or until firm. Rotate dish partway through cooking, if necessary. Let stand on counter and cool completely before cutting into 2 inch (5 cm) squares.

Makes 16 squares

VARIATION
Date or Fig Bars: Combine 2 cups (500 mL) firmly packed chopped dates or figs, ¼ cup (50 mL) granulated sugar, ⅓ cup (75 mL) water and 2 tbsp (25 mL) lemon juice. Follow cooking directions as above.

Jalapeño Cornbread

The small, dark-green jalapeño peppers give a good zip to this cornbread. Use either fresh or canned. Serve with chili.

¾ cup	all-purpose flour	175 mL
¾ cup	cornmeal	175 mL
1 tbsp	granulated sugar	15 mL
1 tbsp	baking powder	15 mL
½ tsp	salt	2 mL
½ tsp	chili powder	2 mL
2	eggs, lightly beaten	2
½ cup	milk	125 mL
¼ cup	vegetable oil	50 mL
¼ cup	chopped jalapeño peppers	50 mL
1 cup	grated old Cheddar cheese	250 mL

▶ Combine flour, cornmeal, sugar, baking powder, salt and chili powder in a large bowl. Set aside.

▶ In a small bowl, stir together eggs, milk, oil, jalapeño peppers and cheese. Pour into dry mixture all at once and stir just until blended. Do not beat.

▶ Pour into lightly greased 9 inch (23 cm) round microwavable baking dish.

▶ Microwave, uncovered, at Medium (50%) for 4 minutes, rotating dish partway through cooking, if necessary. Microwave at High (100%) for 2 to 4 minutes, or until toothpick inserted in several places comes out clean.

▶ Let stand on counter until cool. Cut into wedges.

Makes 12 to 16 servings

TIP To defrost frozen fruit juice quickly, remove the metal cap and microwave at High (100%) for 1 to 3 minutes, or until liquid.

TIP To reheat leftover pancakes or waffles, place two on a microwavable plate. Cover loosely with plastic wrap and microwave at Medium (50%) for 1 to 1½ minutes.

Apple Mincemeat Oatmeal Bars

A good use for any leftover mincemeat—if there is such a thing in your household. The apple cuts the richness of the mincemeat, and the oatmeal provides fiber. This can be served either cool as squares or as a warm crisp with cream or ice cream.

1 cup	all-purpose flour	250 mL
1½ cups	rolled oats	375 mL
½ cup	brown sugar	125 mL
½ tsp	ground nutmeg	2 mL
½ cup	butter, softened	125 mL
1½ cups	mincemeat	375 mL
3	tart apples, peeled, cored and diced	3
½ cup	slivered almonds	125 mL

▶ In medium bowl, combine flour, rolled oats, brown sugar and nutmeg. Cut in butter with a pastry blender or two knives until mixture is crumbly. Press half of mixture evenly in bottom of an 8 inch (20 cm) square glass baking dish.

▶ In medium bowl, combine mincemeat, apples and almonds. Spoon evenly over base. Top with remaining crumb mixture and press evenly.

▶ Microwave, uncovered, at High (100%) for 6 to 8 minutes, or until apples are tender. Rotate dish partway through cooking, if necessary. Cool before cutting into 2 inch (5 cm) squares.

Makes 16 squares

TIP Preparing hot cereal is a one-step process in the microwave, and eliminates a sticky pot to clean. For one serving, combine ¾ cup (175 mL) water, pinch salt and ⅓ cup (75 mL) rolled oats in a deep microwavable 4 cup (1 L) bowl or casserole to prevent boilovers. Microwave, uncovered, at High (100%) for 2 to 4 minutes, or until thick, stirring once. Stand briefly before serving. For quick-cooking oats, use the same amounts but microwave for only 1 to 2 minutes at High (100%).

11
Desserts

The microwave oven does an effortless job of poaching fruit, making light custards such as a sabayon, melting chocolate for a rich mousse, and more.

Conventional recipes that use either a double boiler or a *bain marie* (water bath) to gently set, melt or mold can be adapted easily to the microwave. A lower power setting and a watchful eye produce spectacular results. With a crème caramel, for example, all the steps can be made in the microwave—making the caramel, scalding the milk and baking the custard. Sponge puddings can be baked in the microwave in less than one-quarter the time, and without the hassle of the *bain marie*.

The ease, quick cooking and delicious results of microwave cooking will have you making decadent desserts more often.

Chocolate Fondue

A dessert fondue makes a casual but delicious ending to a meal. Use pieces of fruit and pound cake for dipping.

6 oz	good-quality bittersweet or semisweet chocolate	180 g
½ cup	light cream	125 mL
2 tbsp	corn syrup	25 mL
2 tbsp	brandy, Kahlua, Grand Marnier or Cointreau	25 mL
1 tsp	vanilla	5 mL
	Dippers—sliced bananas, apples, orange segments, strawberries, cherries, grapes or cubes of pound cake	

▶ Combine chocolate and cream in a 4 cup (1 L) casserole. Microwave, uncovered, at High (100%) for 2 to 4 minutes, or until chocolate melts and mixture is smooth. Stir twice during cooking.

▶ Stir in corn syrup, brandy and vanilla until mixture is smooth and glossy. Transfer to a fondue dish set over a burner or candle to keep warm, or reheat as needed to keep warm and fluid—use Medium (50%) when reheating.

▶ Provide long-handled forks and prepared fruit and/or cake for dipping.

Makes 4 servings

Crème Caramel

The microwave oven can often replace the double boiler and the bain marie (water bath). This traditional dessert can now be made in a quarter of the time, using fewer dishes, and the flavor and texture are just as wonderful as with conventional cooking.

¾ cup	granulated sugar	175 mL
2 tbsp	water	25 mL
4	eggs	4
½ tsp	vanilla	2 mL
2 cups	milk	500 mL

▶ In a heavy round 6 cup (1.5 L) glass casserole (not plastic), combine ½ cup (125 mL) sugar and water. Microwave, uncovered, at High (100%) for 4 to 5 minutes, until sugar caramelizes to a golden brown (the color of maple syrup). Do not stir during this time.

▶ With pot holders, remove casserole from oven and rotate dish so caramel coats the sides as well as the bottom. Set aside to cool and harden, about 15 minutes.

▶ In separate bowl, lightly beat eggs with a fork. Blend in remaining sugar and vanilla.

▶ In a 2 cup (500 mL) glass measure, microwave milk at High (100%) for 3 to 4 minutes, or until very hot but not boiling. Stir slowly into egg mixture. Pour over cooled caramel.

▶ Cover with casserole lid or plastic wrap. Microwave at Medium-Low (30%) for 10 to 14 minutes, or until a knife inserted in center comes out clean.

▶ Let stand, covered, and cool to room temperature. Serve warm or refrigerate until serving time.

▶ To serve, place a serving plate with rim over casserole and quickly turn crème caramel out of dish.

Makes 4 to 6 servings

VARIATION: To make individual crème caramels, make caramel in a heavy 2 cup (500 mL) glass measure or bowl and divide between 4 to 6 small microwavable ramekins or custard cups. Let cool and harden. Continue with recipe, dividing custard mixture between ramekins. Arrange in a ring formation in microwave oven, cover and microwave at Medium-Low (30%) for 12 to 16 minutes, or until set. It may be necessary to rearrange ramekins during cooking.

Chilled Lime Clouds

The texture of this dessert is light and airy, and the taste is refreshing. Serve this in attractive wine glasses after a heavy meal. Garnish with thin slices of lime and fresh mint sprigs.

1 cup	granulated sugar	250 mL
¼ cup	cornstarch	50 mL
pinch	salt	pinch
1 cup	unsweetened orange juice	250 mL
	Grated rind and juice of 2 limes, about ½ cup (125 mL) juice	
2	eggs, separated	2
½ tsp	vanilla	2 mL
1 to 2 drops	green food coloring, optional	1 to 2
	Lime slices and fresh mint for garnish	

▶ In an 8 cup (2 L) glass measure or microwavable casserole, combine sugar, cornstarch, salt, orange and lime juices and grated lime rind. Microwave, uncovered, at High (100%) for 5 to 6 minutes, or until mixture comes to a boil and thickens. Beat every 2 minutes during cooking time.

▶ In small bowl or cup, lightly beat egg yolks. Stir a little of hot mixture into eggs, then stir eggs back into mixture. Microwave, uncovered, at High (100%) for 1 minute. Cool to room temperature. Stir in vanilla and green food coloring.

▶ In medium bowl, beat egg whites until stiff but not dry. Gently blend about one-quarter of the egg whites into the lime mixture to lighten the texture. Then carefully fold in the remaining egg whites. Spoon into serving glasses. Refrigerate for several hours until set. Garnish with lime slices and sprig of mint.

Makes 6 servings

Lemon Sponge Pudding

A traditional recipe that eliminates the need for a water bath when cooked in the microwave. It also cooks in far less time. It is a light cake floating on top of a lemony custard— just right after a heavy meal.

2 tbsp	butter, softened	25 mL
¾ cup	granulated sugar	175 mL
3	eggs, separated	3
	Grated rind of ½ lemon	
¼ cup	all-purpose flour	50 mL
¼ tsp	salt	1 mL
1 cup	milk	250 mL
¼ cup	lemon juice	50 mL

▶ In large bowl, cream together butter, sugar, egg yolks and lemon rind until light.

▶ In separate bowl, combine flour and salt. Add alternately to creamed mixture with milk and lemon juice.

▶ In medium bowl, beat egg whites until stiff but not dry. Gently fold into batter.

▶ Pour into a 6 cup (1.5 L) round microwavable casserole. Microwave, uncovered, at Medium (50%) for 6 to 9 minutes, or until top of cake is dry and set. Rotate dish, if necessary, during cooking. Let stand for 5 minutes before serving. Serve warm.

Makes 4 to 6 servings

TIP Warming egg whites will increase the volume when whipped. Place in a microwavable bowl and microwave two egg whites at Medium (50%) for 20 seconds.

TIP Freeze leftover egg whites in a small glass jar to use later for meringues or cakes. They will keep for 12 months in the freezer. Defrost in the microwave and use 1 tbsp (15 mL) for each egg white required in a recipe.

Mandarin and Chocolate Cream Pie

The mandarin filling is refreshing and is wonderful when combined with the chocolate.

¼ cup	butter	50 mL
2 tbsp	granulated sugar	25 mL
1¼ cups	chocolate wafer crumbs or chocolate Graham cracker crumbs	300 mL
½ cup	granulated sugar	125 mL
¼ cup	cornstarch	50 mL
1½ cups	unsweetened orange juice	375 mL
1 tsp	vanilla	5 mL
2	10 oz (284 mL) cans whole mandarin orange segments, well drained	2
½ cup	whipping cream	125 mL

▶ Melt butter in a 9 inch (23 cm) glass pie plate at High (100%) for 1 to 1½ minutes. Stir in 2 tbsp (25 mL) sugar and crumbs until evenly coated with butter. Press onto bottom and sides of dish.

▶ Microwave at High (100%) for 2 to 3 minutes, or until firm. Rotate dish, if necessary, during cooking. Cool, then refrigerate.

▶ Meanwhile, make filling by combining ½ cup (125 mL) sugar and cornstarch in an 8 cup (2 L) glass measure or microwavable casserole. Stir in orange juice until smooth. Microwave, uncovered, at High (100%) for 4 to 6 minutes, or until mixture comes to a boil and thickens. Beat every 2 minutes with a wire whisk for a smooth mixture. Let cool to room temperature.

▶ When cool, stir in vanilla and fold in mandarin oranges.

▶ In separate bowl, whip cream until stiff. Stir about one-quarter of the whipped cream into the orange mixture. Fold in remaining whipped cream. Spoon into pie shell and chill for several hours. Garnish with chocolate curls (page 180).

Makes 6 to 8 servings

Grand Marnier Cheesecake in Orange Cups

Use the oranges as the serving containers, for an attractive presentation. In the microwave they will retain their color and firmness.

8	oranges, about 2½ inches (6 cm) in diameter	8
8 oz	cream cheese, softened	250 g
½ cup	granulated sugar	125 mL
2	eggs	2
½ cup	sour cream	125 mL
2 tbsp	Grand Marnier	25 mL
1 tsp	vanilla	5 mL
½ cup	whipping cream	125 mL

▶ Cut the top quarter off oranges. If necessary, trim bottom of each orange so they will stand up. Make sure you do not cut through to the pulp.

▶ Remove pulp from orange halves with a serrated grapefruit knife, reserving pulp from one orange for filling. (Save remaining fruit for breakfast!) Be careful not to cut through skin when cleaning out oranges.

▶ In medium bowl, beat cream cheese with sugar, then beat in eggs one at a time. Chop the reserved pulp from one orange and blend into cream cheese mixture with sour cream, Grand Marnier and vanilla.

▶ Divide mixture between the 8 orange cups, filling only about three-quarters full (mixture will puff up during cooking). Arrange in a ring formation in microwave and microwave, uncovered, at Medium (50%) for 10 to 14 minutes, until fillings are almost set. Rotate and rearrange orange cups partway through cooking, if necessary. Do not overcook, or cheese will toughen.

▶ Cool completely at room temperature, then chill until serving. To serve, whip cream and pipe on top of each orange cup.

Makes 8 servings

Poached Peaches and Plums with Orange Sabayon

A sabayon is a foamy custard that is served warm. You can poach the fruit up to two hours ahead of time, but make the custard at the last minute.

6	firm but ripe peaches	6
6	firm but ripe plums	6
⅓ cup	orange liqueur, apricot brandy or peach schnapps	75 mL
3	egg yolks	3
⅓ cup	granulated sugar	75 mL

▶ Quarter peaches and plums and remove pits. If you prefer, peel fruit.

▶ Combine peaches and liqueur in an 8 cup (2 L) microwavable casserole. Cover and microwave at High (100%) for 2 minutes.

▶ Gently stir in plums and microwave at High (100%) for 4 to 5 minutes, or until fruit is almost tender. Let stand for 10 minutes, then pour off and reserve poaching liquid.

▶ Chill fruit until serving time. Keep poaching liquid at room temperature.

▶ In a 6 cup (1.5 L) microwavable bowl, beat egg yolks and sugar with an electric beater until thick and lemon-colored. Beat in reserved poaching liquid.

▶ Microwave, uncovered, at Medium (50%) for 4 to 6 minutes, beating every minute with a wire whisk, until custard is thick and creamy.

▶ Divide fruit between serving dishes and spoon custard over top. Serve immediately.

Makes 6 to 8 servings

Poached Peaches
with Blueberry Sauce

Use fresh peaches in season for this attractive, delicious, yet quick dessert. If you use canned peaches, omit the poaching step and the sugar, and use the canned syrup for the poaching liquid.

4	firm but ripe peaches	4
¼ cup	Cointreau	50 mL
½ cup	granulated sugar	125 mL
2 tbsp	cornstarch	25 mL
1 cup	blueberries or raspberries	250 mL
1 tbsp	lemon juice	15 mL

▶ Peel and halve peaches. Place in a shallow 10 inch (25 cm) microwavable dish with Cointreau. Cover with lid or plastic wrap and microwave at Medium (50%) for 4 to 5 minutes, or until peaches are tender.

▶ Cool peaches for 15 minutes. Drain and reserve liquid. Set peaches aside.

▶ In a 4 cup (1 L) glass measure, combine sugar and cornstarch. Stir in reserved poaching liquid until smooth. Stir in blueberries.

▶ Microwave, uncovered, at High (100%) for 4 to 5 minutes, or until mixture comes to a boil and thickens. Stir at least once partway through cooking. Stir in lemon juice and cool.

▶ To serve, place two peaches halves in each serving dish. Pour sauce over peaches.

Makes 4 servings

TIP To dissolve unflavored gelatin, sprinkle gelatin over the liquid as specified in the recipe and let stand for a few minutes to soften. Microwave at Medium (50%) for 30 to 60 seconds per envelope, or until dissolved.

Rich Tart Shells
with Warm Fruit Filling

These oversized tart shells are shortbread-like in flavor, and the
brown sugar gives them an attractive color. Roll the pastry thin
for delicate shells. The filling is not only beautiful,
but delicious served warm.

TART PASTRY

⅓ cup	butter	75 mL
⅓ cup	brown sugar	75 mL
1	egg	1
½ tsp	vanilla	2 mL
1½ cups	all-purpose flour	375 mL
¼ tsp	salt	1 mL

FILLING

2	oranges	2
2	kiwi fruit	2
1 tbsp	cornstarch	15 mL
⅓ cup	granulated sugar	75 mL
1 cup	water	250 mL
½ cup	seedless green grapes	125 mL
2 tbsp	Cointreau or Grand Marnier	25 mL
1 cup	strawberries	250 mL

▶ In a medium microwavable bowl, soften butter at Medium (50%) for 20 to 40 seconds. Beat in brown sugar until creamy. Beat in egg, then vanilla until fluffy and smooth.

▶ In separate bowl, combine flour and salt. Gradually stir into butter-egg mixture. Form dough into a ball and wrap in plastic wrap. Chill for at least 30 minutes—it will be easier to roll.

▶ Divide dough in half. Cut two pieces of plastic wrap about 12 inches (30 cm) long. Place one piece of dough between sheets of plastic wrap and roll out until about ¹⁄₁₆ inch (3 mm) thick. Remove top sheet of plastic wrap. Cut three rounds about 4½ inches (12 cm) in diameter. Repeat with remaining dough.

▶ Invert six 6 oz (175 mL) custard cups. Cover the bottoms with white paper towels, then the pastry rounds. Gently pinch the edges in five places so pastry molds to edge of cups.

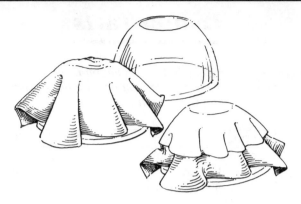

▶ In microwave, arrange cups in ring formation. Microwave at Medium-High (70%) for 6 to 8 minutes, or until cups are firm and the greasy look has disappeared. Rotate cups, if necessary, during cooking. Let stand for 5 minutes, then remove paper towels and invert tart shells to cool.

▶ Peel and cut oranges into small pieces. Peel and cut kiwi into quarters.

▶ Combine cornstarch, sugar and water in a 4 cup (1 L) glass measure or microwavable bowl. Microwave, uncovered, at High (100%) for 3 to 5 minutes, or until mixture comes to a boil and thickens. Stir twice during cooking.

▶ Add oranges, kiwi and grapes to cornstarch mixture. Microwave at High (100%), for 1 to 2 minutes or until warm. Stir in liqueur. (The filling can be prepared ahead to this point, then reheated just before serving.)

▶ To serve, slice strawberries and fold into warm fruit mixture. Spoon filling into tart shells.

Makes 6 servings

TIP To soften a gelatin mixture that has set before you've added the fruit or vegetables, microwave at Medium (50%) until liquid again.

Lemon Tarts

Lemon curd makes a wonderfully rich lemon filling for tarts. Fill the baked tart shells after the lemon curd has cooled, and serve soon after filling.

3	eggs	3
¾ cup	granulated sugar	175 mL
¼ cup	fresh lemon juice	50 mL
	Grated rind of ½ lemon	
¼ cup	butter, cut into small pieces	50 mL
12	2 inch (5 cm) baked tart shells	12

▶ In a 4 cup (1 L) glass measure or microwavable casserole, lightly beat eggs. Beat in sugar, lemon juice and rind until smooth.
▶ Microwave, uncovered, at Medium (50%) for 5 to 7 minutes, or until mixture thickens. Beat every 2 minutes.
▶ Gradually beat in butter a little at a time, making sure each addition has melted before adding the next. Refrigerate filling until cool (mixture will thicken as it cools).
▶ Fill baked tart shells with cooled filling and serve.

Makes 12 tarts

Rich Chocolate Orange Mousse

Serve this rich dessert in sherbet glasses and garnish with Candied Fruit Peel (page 186). Or use as a filling for chocolate shells (page 178).

6 oz	good-quality bittersweet or semisweet chocolate	180 g
¼ cup	butter, softened	50 mL
	Grated rind of 1 orange	
2	eggs, lightly beaten	2
¼ cup	granulated sugar	50 mL
2 tbsp	orange liqueur	25 mL
1 cup	whipping cream	250 mL

▶ In a 6 cup (1.5 L) microwavable casserole, melt the chocolate at Medium (50%) for 3 to 5 minutes, stirring partway through to help melt chocolate. Stir in butter until melted, then stir in orange rind.

▶ In small bowl, beat eggs and sugar together until thick and lemon-colored. Stir into chocolate mixture until smooth. Stir in liqueur.

▶ In separate bowl, beat whipping cream until stiff. Stir about one-quarter of whipped cream into chocolate mixture to lighten. Then fold remaining whipped cream into chocolate mixture until evenly blended.

▶ Spoon into serving glasses and chill until set, about 2 hours.

Makes 6 servings

Cranberry Apple Crisp

A dessert to make in the fall or winter, when apples and cranberries are plentiful. Serve this warm with ice cream or Crème Anglaise (page 142).

1 cup	rolled oats	250 mL
½ cup	all-purpose flour	125 mL
⅓ cup	brown sugar	75 mL
¼ cup	butter, softened	50 mL
4	cooking apples, peeled, cored and cut into eighths	4
1 cup	cranberries, washed and picked over	250 mL
	Grated rind of ½ orange	

▶ In medium bowl, combine rolled oats, flour and brown sugar. Blend in butter until mixture is crumbly.

▶ Arrange apple slices evenly on the bottom of a 6 cup (1.5 L) microwavable casserole or baking dish. Sprinkle cranberries, then orange rind, over apples. Top with crumb topping.

▶ Microwave, uncovered, at High (100%) for 6 to 8 minutes, or until apples are tender. Rotate dish, if necessary, during cooking.

Makes 6 servings

Pear and Ginger Hazelnut Crumble

The preserved ginger gives an interesting flavor to the pears, and makes this homey dessert special enough for guests. Serve warm with ice cream, whipped cream or Crème Anglaise (page 142).

6	firm but ripe pears	6
1 tbsp	lemon juice	15 mL
¼ cup	brown sugar	50 mL
2 tbsp	all-purpose flour	25 mL
½ tsp	ground nutmeg	2 mL
4 or 5	pieces preserved ginger, chopped	4 or 5
1 cup	rolled oats	250 mL
½ cup	chopped toasted hazelnuts (see below)	125 mL
⅓ cup	brown sugar	75 mL
¼ cup	butter, softened	50 mL

▶ Peel, core and slice pears into eighths lengthwise. Place in medium bowl and sprinkle with lemon juice.

▶ In small bowl, combine ¼ cup (50 mL) brown sugar, flour and nutmeg. Sprinkle over pears and toss lightly to coat.

▶ Arrange pears in a 9 inch (23 cm) round microwavable baking dish or casserole. Sprinkle ginger evenly over pears.

▶ In medium bowl, combine rolled oats, chopped hazelnuts and ⅓ cup (75 mL) brown sugar. Blend in butter until mixture is crumbly, then spread evenly over fruit.

▶ Microwave, uncovered, at High (100%) for 6 to 8 minutes, or until pears are tender. Rotate dish, if necessary, during cooking.

Makes 6 to 8 servings

TIP Toast nuts or coconut by spreading out on a microwavable plate. Microwave at High (100%) for 2 to 4 minutes per ½ cup (125 mL), or until lightly toasted. Stir or shake dish often to prevent burning.

Maple Pecan Tarts

These tarts are a cross between the all-Canadian butter tart and Southern pecan pie, but with the rich flavor of maple syrup. The tart shells are baked conventionally—make your own pastry or bake frozen ones.

1 cup	chopped pecans	250 mL
2 tbsp	butter	25 mL
3	eggs	3
½ cup	brown sugar	125 mL
½ cup	pure maple syrup	125 mL
1 tsp	vanilla	5 mL
½ tsp	maple extract	2 mL
2 tbsp	all-purpose flour	25 mL
pinch	salt	pinch
24	2 inch (5 cm) baked tart shells	24

▶ Spread nuts on a glass pie plate. Microwave, uncovered, at High (100%) for 2 to 4 minutes, or until toasted. Shake or stir partway through cooking and watch nuts carefully to avoid burning.
▶ In small microwavable dish or measuring cup, microwave butter at High (100%) for 30 to 60 seconds, or until melted.
▶ In medium bowl, beat eggs well. Add nuts, melted butter and all remaining ingredients except tart shells, blending well after each addition.
▶ Arrange six baked tart shells in a ring formation on a microwave roasting rack. Spoon about 2 tbsp (25 mL) filling into each shell. Microwave, uncovered, at Medium (50%) for 2 to 3 minutes, or just until set. Remove from rack and cool. Repeat with remaining tarts, six at a time.

Makes 24 tarts

TIP To soften marzipan (almond paste), microwave 4 oz (125 g) at High (100%) for 10 to 15 seconds before rolling or molding.

Apple Custard Flan

Nothing satisfies like a warm dessert in winter. This one is neither too sweet nor too filling, but it's so delicious that there won't be any leftovers.

4	cooking apples	4
¼ cup	dark rum	50 mL
2 cups	Crème Anglaise (page 142)	500 mL
½ cup	slivered almonds	125 mL
2 tbsp	butter	25 mL
2 tbsp	granulated sugar	25 mL

▶ Peel and quarter apples. Arrange in an even pattern in a 9 inch (23 cm) microwavable quiche or flan dish. Pour rum over apples. (This helps to keep the apples from turning brown.)

▶ Cover with waxed paper and microwave at High (100%) for 4 to 6 minutes, or until apples are tender. Set aside.

▶ Make Crème Anglaise and pour over apples.

▶ In a small microwavable bowl, combine almonds, butter and sugar. Microwave, uncovered, at High (100%) for 2 to 4 minutes, or until butter is melted and nuts are lightly toasted. Stir often and watch carefully, as nuts can burn very quickly.

▶ Sprinkle nuts over apples and sauce before serving. Serve warm or cool.

Makes 4 to 6 servings

TIP Cake cones can be easily made by spooning 2 tbsp (25 mL) cake batter into flat-bottomed ice cream cones. Arrange in a ring formation in microwave oven and microwave at High (100%) for 10 to 20 seconds each, or until a toothpick inserted in the center of the batter comes out clean.

Chocolate Tips

▶ Melting chocolate in the microwave eliminates the need for double boilers, boiling water and a messy kitchen. It also saves time.
▶ Chocolate can be easily scorched by overcooking. When working with chocolate in the microwave, use Medium power (50%), stir to help melting, and don't overcook.
▶ In the microwave, fully melted chocolate can very deceivingly hold its shape. The last small pieces should be melted by stirring.
▶ If you are melting chocolate with another ingredient such as milk or butter, you can use High power (100%), but otherwise use Medium (50%) and stir often.
▶ Not all chocolate is created equal. Use the type called for in the recipe. For both flavor and quality, use "real" chocolate, not chocolate-flavored substitutes.

Chocolate Cups

▶ Melt semisweet or bittersweet chocolate in a microwavable bowl at Medium (50%)—about 2 minutes per ounce (30 g). Using a small brush, carefully brush chocolate on the insides of small paper or foil cups. Make a fairly thick layer—if too thin, the chocolate will break. Refrigerate or freeze until firm. Then carefully peel the paper away from the chocolate. Refrigerate the cups until ready to fill.

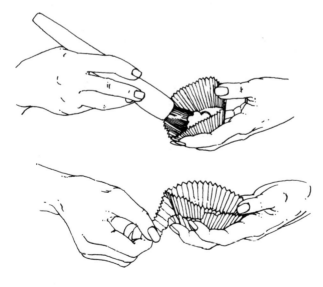

Chocolate Pie Shell

▶ Only with the microwave can you make this nifty chocolate shell as a base for pies, mousses or ice cream. Line a 9 inch (23 cm) glass plate with a large piece of plastic wrap. Smooth out the plastic as much as possible. Place 1 cup (250 mL) chocolate chips or chopped bittersweet chocolate in the lined plate. Microwave at Medium (50%) for 3 to 4 minutes, stirring gently partway through cooking to help melt chocolate.

▶ Spread the melted chocolate over the bottom and sides of the plate until it forms a shell. If the chocolate is too runny, let it cool slightly before spreading. Make as even a layer as possible—thin areas may break when you remove the plastic wrap.

▶ Refrigerate until very firm, then carefully remove the shell from the plate by lifting the plastic wrap. Gently peel the wrap away from the chocolate. Work quickly but carefully, as the heat of your hands will melt the chocolate. If you have time, melt a little more chocolate in a separate bowl and add another layer of chocolate to the sides of the refrigerated shell. Again refrigerate until firm. This will add strength to the particularly delicate sides.

▶ Replace the chocolate shell in the pie plate and refrigerate until ready to fill.

▶ Fill chocolate shells or cups with Chilled Lime Clouds (page 164), the filling for Mandarin and Chocolate Cream Pie (page 166), or Rich Chocolate Orange Mousse (page 172).

▶ Very small chocolate cups can be filled with liqueur and served as an elegant end to a meal. Fill a coffee cup three-quarters full of hot coffee. Gently place a liqueur-filled chocolate cup in the coffee and enjoy.

▶ Fill chocolate cups with fresh raspberries or strawberries and place three cups in a pool of raspberry or strawberry sauce on a dessert plate. To make a sauce, puree and sieve fresh berries. Flavor with sugar and liqueur to taste.

Chocolate Garnishes

Chocolate-dipped Fruit

▶ Melt semisweet or bittersweet chocolate in a microwavable bowl at Medium (50%). Wash and completely dry fruit (strawberries, cherries, grapes, mandarin or orange segments, etc.). Dip fruit in melted chocolate about halfway up the fruit. Gently shake off any excess and transfer to waxed paper to cool and harden.

Chocolate Leaves

▶ Melt semisweet or bittersweet chocolate and use a small brush to paint a thin layer of melted chocolate on the back of small washed and dried non-toxic leaves. Leaves from a rose or an orange plant are ideal. Place on a plate and refrigerate until firm.
▶ Carefully peel leaves away from chocolate and refrigerate until ready to use. For contrast, make both white and dark chocolate leaves to garnish desserts.

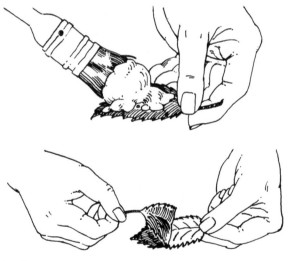

Chocolate Cutouts

▶ Melt semisweet or bittersweet chocolate and pour on a baking sheet lined with waxed paper. Smooth to a ⅛ inch (3 mm) thickness with a smooth knife or a spoon. Refrigerate until firm, then cut out shapes with sharp cookie cutters, or use a small sharp knife to make wedges or triangles. Peel paper off cutouts and chill until using.

Chocolate Rolls

▶ Melt and spread chocolate on a waxed paper-lined baking sheet. Chill until set, then peel off paper and cut into rectangles about 2½ × 1½ inches (6 × 3 cm). Work quickly to roll rectangles around handle of wooden spoon. Slip onto a plate when rolled. The trick is having the chocolate at just the right temperature. If it is too hard, it will crack; if it is too soft, it will stick to the spoon. Let stand at room temperature to soften; chill to harden.

Chocolate Curls

▶ Soften 1 square of semisweet chocolate at Medium-Low (30%) for 3 to 6 seconds, then shave off curls with a vegetable peeler.

Chocolate Tracings

▶ Spoon melted chocolate into a piping bag. Designs can be piped directly onto cookies or cakes. To trace shapes, place waxed paper over illustration and trace outline. Refrigerate until firm, then remove waxed paper. Make initials for a birthday cake or Christmas shapes to hang on the tree.

12
Gifts from the Kitchen, and More

Nothing says "thank you" or "I care" quite like a personally made gift—particularly one from the kitchen. The microwave is handy for making chocolate truffles, candies, seasoned nuts, sauces and even a terrific hot mustard. These can all be last-minute gifts, as they are prepared and cooked so quickly.

Package your gifts attractively in pretty containers, jars or bottles and tie on a bow. Add usage or heating instructions on the gift card. Don't overlook recipes in other chapters as gift ideas, such as Creamy Salad Dressing (page 136), or any of the luscious dessert sauces, cakes or squares.

Lemonade Concentrate

A special treat on a hot summer day.
Fill a pitcher with it along with orange and lemon slices.
This concentrate also makes a nice base for vodka or gin.

6	lemons	6
1 cup	granulated sugar	250 mL
½ cup	water	125 mL

▶ Remove rind from 1 lemon with potato peeler, being careful not to include any of the white pith, which can add a bitter flavor.
▶ Squeeze juice from all lemons into a 4 cup (1 L) glass measure. Add rind, sugar and water. Cover with vented plastic wrap and microwave at High (100%) for 2 to 4 minutes, or until mixture comes to a boil. Cool, strain and store in refrigerator.
▶ Use about 2 tbsp (25 mL) concentrate for every large glass of water. (Soda water will give it sparkle.) Pour over ice.

Makes enough for fifteen 7 oz (200 mL) glasses

Hot and Sweet Mustard

A great mustard for sandwiches, to flavor salad dressings, or for any recipe where a Russian-style mustard is called for.

1 cup	dry mustard	250 mL
¼ tsp	freshly ground white pepper	1 mL
¼ tsp	paprika	1 mL
¾ cup	granulated sugar	175 mL
1 tsp	salt	5 mL
1 cup	white wine	250 mL
3 tbsp	white vinegar	50 mL
2	egg yolks	2

▶ In a 4 cup (1 L) glass measure, combine mustard, pepper, paprika, sugar and salt. Add wine and vinegar and combine well.
▶ Microwave, uncovered, at High (100%) for 2 to 3 minutes or until bubbles start to form on the top. Stir after 1 minute of cooking time.
▶ In separate bowl, beat egg yolks. Slowly add about ½ cup (125 mL) hot mixture to the egg yolks. Return the egg mixture to the hot mustard and whisk well.
▶ Microwave, uncovered, at Medium (50%) for 2 to 3 minutes, or until mixture thickens. Whisk twice during cooking.
▶ Pour into clean jars. Refrigerate and use within two months.

Makes 2 cups (500 mL)

VARIATIONS
Tarragon Mustard: Stir 1 tbsp (15 mL) dried tarragon into cooked mustard.

Green Peppercorn Mustard: Stir 1 tbsp (15 mL) crushed, pickled green peppercorns into mustard.

TIP Lemons, oranges and limes yield more juice when slightly warm. Microwave each at High (100%) for 15 seconds. Cut in half and squeeze.

A Trio of Truffles

Decadent truffles are as simple to make in the microwave as melting chocolate. Use a good-quality imported chocolate for the best flavor. Try one or all three recipes, as they look attractive together with the different coatings. To freeze, arrange the truffles in a single layer in a shallow plastic freezer container. Defrost in the refrigerator.

Amaretto Truffles

6 oz	white chocolate	180 g
¾ cup	ground almonds	175 mL
¼ cup	butter, softened	50 mL
¼ cup	icing sugar	50 mL
½ tsp	almond extract	2 mL
2 tbsp	Amaretto (almond liqueur)	25 mL

▶ Melt chocolate in a 6 cup (1.5 L) microwavable bowl, uncovered, at Medium (50%) for 4 to 5 minutes, stirring often to help melt chocolate.

▶ Stir ¼ cup (50 mL) ground almonds into chocolate. Beat in butter, 1 tbsp (15 mL) at a time, until melted and smooth. Stir in icing sugar, almond extract and Amaretto until evenly blended.

▶ Refrigerate until firm enough to shape, 1 to 2 hours. Shape in small balls and roll in remaining ground almonds to coat. Place in small paper candy cups. Keep refrigerated or freeze.

▶ Remove from refrigerator about 20 minutes before serving.

Makes 30 to 36 truffles

Chocolate Hazelnut Truffles

1 cup	hazelnuts	250 mL
6 oz	good-quality bittersweet or semisweet chocolate	180 g
¼ cup	butter, softened	50 mL
¼ cup	icing sugar	50 mL
2 tbsp	Frangelico (hazelnut liqueur)	25 mL

▶ Spread hazelnuts out on a large shallow plate such as a glass pie plate. Microwave, uncovered, at High (100%) for 2 to 4 minutes, or until lightly toasted. Stir often and watch carefully, as nuts can easily burn. Rub nuts in a clean, dry tea towel to remove as much of the skin as possible. Process nuts in food processor until very finely chopped. Set aside.

▶ Melt chocolate in a 6 cup (1.5 L) microwavable bowl, uncovered, at Medium (50%) for 4 to 5 minutes, stirring often to help melt chocolate. (Chocolate tends to hold its shape when melted in the microwave.)

▶ Stir ¼ cup (50 mL) toasted ground hazelnuts into chocolate.

▶ Beat in butter 1 tbsp (15 mL) at a time, until melted and smooth. Stir in icing sugar and Frangelico until evenly blended.

▶ Refrigerate mixture until firm enough to shape, 1 to 2 hours. Shape in small balls and roll in the remaining finely ground toasted hazelnuts. Place in small paper candy cups. Keep refrigerated or freeze.

▶ Remove from refrigerator about 20 minutes before serving.

Makes 30 to 36 truffles

Mocha Truffles

6 oz	good-quality bittersweet or semisweet chocolate	180 g
1 tsp	instant coffee powder	5 mL
¼ cup	butter, softened	50 mL
¼ cup	icing sugar	50 mL
2 tbsp	Kahlua or Tia Maria (coffee liqueur)	25 mL
½ cup	cocoa powder	125 mL

▶ Melt chocolate in a 6 cup (1.5 L) microwavable bowl, uncovered, at Medium (50%) for 4 to 5 minutes, stirring often to help melt chocolate.

▶ Stir instant coffee into chocolate until dissolved. Beat in butter, 1 tbsp (15 mL) at a time, until melted and smooth. Stir in icing sugar and Kahlua until evenly blended.

▶ Refrigerate until firm enough to shape, 1 to 2 hours. Shape in small balls and roll in cocoa powder to coat. Place in small paper candy cups. Keep refrigerated or freeze.

▶ Remove from refrigerator about 20 minutes before serving.

Makes 30 to 36 truffles

Candied Fruit Peel

Delicious on its own, as a garnish or a gift, candied fruit peel also adds flavor to hot coffee, tea or chocolate. It will keep for about one month when stored in an airtight container.

3	large oranges	3
1	lemon	1
	Water	
1¼ cups	granulated sugar	300 mL
½ tsp	ground ginger	2 mL

▶ With a potato peeler, remove rind from oranges and lemon in thin ½ inch (1 cm) strips. Do not include the bitter white pith.

▶ In a heavy glass 8 cup (2 L) casserole with lid, combine rind and 2 cups (500 mL) water. Cover and microwave at High (100%) for 5 to 7 minutes, or until water boils. Drain the strips and repeat the process twice more to remove the bitter oils.

▶ Combine ⅓ cup (75 mL) water, 1 cup (250 mL) sugar and ginger in the same casserole. Stir in rind. Microwave, uncovered, at High (100%) for 8 to 10 minutes, or until rind is transparent and soft. Stir every 3 minutes. Set aside until cool enough to handle.

▶ Sprinkle remaining ¼ cup (50 mL) sugar evenly over waxed paper-lined baking sheet. Remove peel from syrup a few pieces at a time and coat lightly in sugar. Transfer to a wire rack and allow to cool and dry completely, at least 6 to 8 hours or overnight. Store in an airtight container.

Makes about 1 cup (250 mL)

Praline

A crunchy topping for ice cream or other desserts. Almonds or pecans can be substituted for the hazelnuts.

½ cup	granulated sugar	125 mL
2 tbsp	water	25 mL
½ cup	whole hazelnuts, almonds or pecans	125 mL

▶ Lightly oil a cookie sheet.

▶ In a 4 cup (1 L) heavy glass measure, combine sugar and water, stirring to blend. Stir in nuts.

▶ Microwave, uncovered, at High (100%) for 6 to 8 minutes, or until mixture becomes a chestnut-brown color. Watch carefully but do not stir. Pour onto prepared cookie sheet and cool.

▶ When hardened, break up with a rolling pin or crush in a food processor. Store in an airtight container.

Makes ¾ cup (175 mL)

Peanut Brittle

A microwave candy thermometer would be useful when making this candy, though the best and easiest gauge is your eye and proper timing. When the mixture is a light golden brown, it's ready.

1 cup	granulated sugar	250 mL
½ cup	corn syrup	125 mL
1½ cups	roasted salted peanuts	375 mL
1 tbsp	butter	15 mL
1 tsp	baking soda	5 mL
1 tsp	vanilla	5 mL

▶ Heavily butter a baking sheet.

▶ In an 8 cup (2 L) heavy glass measure or casserole, combine sugar and corn syrup. Microwave, uncovered, at High (100%) for 4 minutes.

▶ Stir in peanuts and microwave at High (100%) for 3 to 5 minutes, or until mixture is light brown and reaches hard crack stage (candy forms a hard brittle thread when dropped into a glass of cold water)—300 F (150 C) on a candy thermometer.

▶ Quickly stir in butter, baking soda and vanilla until light and foamy. Spread as thinly as possible on buttered baking sheet.

▶ Let cool for about 1 hour, then break into pieces. Store in an airtight container.

Makes 1 lb (500 g)

Sponge Toffee

The original sponge toffee—the kind that sticks in your teeth! This toffee is best eaten the day it's made and, like most candy, it is best made when the humidity is low. A microwave candy thermometer would be useful, although a conventional candy thermometer can be used outside the microwave.

1 cup	granulated sugar	250 mL
1 cup	corn syrup	250 mL
1 tbsp	white vinegar	15 mL
1 tbsp	baking soda	15 mL

▶ Line an 8 inch (20 cm) square pan with foil, and butter foil well.
▶ Combine sugar, corn syrup and vinegar in a heavy 8 cup (2 L) glass measure or casserole. Microwave, uncovered, at High (100%) for 3 minutes. Stir well.
▶ Continue to microwave at High (100%) for 6 to 10 minutes, or until the mixture thickens and reaches hard crack stage (candy forms hard brittle thread when dropped into a glass of cold water) or 300 F (150 C) on a candy thermometer. Stir occasionally during cooking.
▶ Quickly stir in baking soda, mixing well. Mixture will foam up. Pour into prepared pan. Let stand until cool and firm, then remove from dish and foil and break into pieces.

Makes 1 lb (500 g)

TIP For easier pouring of corn syrup, honey or molasses, remove the metal cap and microwave at High (100%) for 10 to 20 seconds.

Orange Sugared Pecans

Keep some attractive jars and festive ribbons and bows on hand for this quick last-minute hostess gift.

2 cups	pecan halves	500 mL
1	egg white, lightly beaten	1
¼ cup	brown sugar	50 mL
1 tbsp	grated orange rind	15 mL
½ tsp	cinnamon	2 mL

▶ Place pecans in a glass pie plate or shallow microwavable dish. Add egg white and stir together until nuts are evenly moistened.
▶ In small bowl or cup, combine brown sugar, orange rind and cinnamon. Sprinkle mixture over nuts and toss to coat evenly.
▶ Microwave, uncovered, at High (100%) for 4 to 6 minutes, or until pecans lose their gloss. Stir often during cooking. Let stand until completely cool, then pack into containers.

Makes 2 cups (500 mL)

Candied Almonds

A buttery, sweet confection—easy enough for the kids to make, and delicious enough for gift-giving.

¼ cup	butter	50 mL
2 cups	blanched whole almonds	500 mL
¼ cup	granulated sugar	50 mL

▶ In a large glass pie plate or shallow microwavable dish, melt butter at High (100%) for 40 to 60 seconds. Stir in almonds, then stir in sugar until almonds are evenly coated.
▶ Microwave, uncovered, at High (100%) for 4 to 6 minutes, or until nuts are lightly toasted. Stir often and watch carefully, as nuts can burn quickly.
▶ Let stand until completely cool, then pack into containers.

Makes 2 cups (500 mL)

Nutty Nibblers

A fast snack or appetizer to make in a variety of flavors.
Use your favorite shelled nuts.
Nuts toast easily in the microwave, but need to be spread out on
a shallow dish and stirred occasionally.
Watch them carefully to avoid burning.

1 cup	shelled unsalted nuts—almonds, cashews, hazelnuts, peanuts, pecans or walnuts	250 mL
1 tsp	vegetable oil	5 mL
	Seasoning Mixture (see below)	

▶ In a shallow microwavable dish such as a glass pie plate, toss nuts with oil to coat evenly. Microwave at High (100%) for 3 to 5 minutes, or until lightly toasted. Stir often during cooking.

▶ Sprinkle seasoning mixture over nuts and stir to coat evenly. Microwave, uncovered, at High (100%) for 1 to 2 minutes to blend flavors. Drain on paper towels. Cool.

Makes 1 cup (250 mL)

Seasoning Mixtures
Curry: Mix 1 tsp (5 mL) curry powder, ¼ tsp (1 mL) salt and a pinch of garlic powder.

Mexican: Combine ½ tsp (2 mL) ground cumin with ¼ tsp (1 mL) each chili powder, ground coriander and salt.

Garlic: Shake together ½ tsp (2 mL) garlic powder and ¼ tsp (1 mL) each paprika and salt.

Teriyaki: Stir together 1 tsp (5 mL) soy sauce, ½ tsp (2 mL) ground ginger and ¼ tsp (1 mL) garlic powder.

TIP Freshen stale pretzels, potato chips, chow mein noodles or popcorn. Place in a paper towel-lined wicker basket or plate and microwave at High (100%) for about 30 to 60 seconds, or until barely warmed.

Index

INDEX

INDEX